Baby Read-Aloud Basics

Baby Read-Aloud Basics

FUN AND INTERACTIVE WAYS TO HELP YOUR LITTLE ONE DISCOVER THE WORLD OF WORDS

CAROLINE J. BLAKEMORE & BARBARA WESTON RAMIREZ

AMACOM

AMERICAN MANAGEMENT ASSOCIATION

NEW YORK • ATLANTA • BRUSSELS • CHICAGO • MEXICO CITY • SAN FRANCISCO
SHANGHAI • TOKYO • TORONTO • WASHINGTON, D. C.

Special discounts on bulk quantities of AMACOM books are
available to corporations, professional associations, and other
organizations. For details, contact Special Sales Department,
AMACOM, a division of American Management Association,
1601 Broadway, New York, NY 10019.
Tel.: 212-903-8316. Fax: 212-903-8083.
Web Site: www.amacombooks.org

This publication is designed to provide accurate and authoritative
information in regard to the subject matter covered. It is sold with the
understanding that the publisher is not engaged in rendering legal,
accounting, or other professional service. If legal advice or other expert
assistance is required, the services of a competent professional person
should be sought.

Library of Congress Cataloging-in-Publication Data

Blakemore, Caroline.
    Baby read-aloud basics : fun and interactive ways to help your little one discover
the world of words / Caroline Blakemore and Barbara Weston Ramirez.
        p.   cm.
    Includes bibliographical references and index.
    ISBN-10: 0-8144-7358-X
    ISBN-13: 978-0-8144-7358-0
    1. Reading (Early childhood)   2. Reading (Early childhood)—Parent
participation.   I. Weston-Ramirez, Barbara.   II. Title.

LB1139.5.R43B58   2006
372.4—dc22   2005036273

Hand drawings by Irina Gronborg.
Photos on pages 1, 5, 21, 22, 31, 33, 44, 62, 66, 79, 82, 95, 98, 114,
116, 117, and 133 by Linda Posnick.

Printing number

10   9   8   7   6   5   4   3   2   1

Dedications

From Caroline J. Blakemore:

To my precious students over the past thirty years, who taught me everything I know about what it takes to become a reader; and to my inspiring, book-loving grandchildren, who helped us create this book: Gavin, Sadie, Kaia; and to my soon-to-be-born fourth granddaughter.

From Barbara Weston Ramirez:

To my hard-working students from Mexico and Guatemala, who strive to become bilingual and adapt to a new culture; and to my older son, Fernando, who taught me how to raise a bilingual child; and to my son, Ricardo, who was born during the writing of this book, and became our test baby, and who is now a book lover.

Contents

Acknowledgments

When Caroline saw her tiny, tiny two-months premature grandson, Gavin, in the Neonatal Intensive Care Unit (NICU) enveloped in his mother's arms while she read him a baby book, Barbara and Caroline thought of their dear students, most of whom had rarely, if at all, been read to. We asked ourselves, "What if all babies received the kind of loving attention Gavin was getting through the attentive words he was hearing day in and day out from his devoted parents? How would reading aloud to babies from birth bring joy and abundance of all kinds into their lives?" *Baby Read-Aloud Basics* is the result of asking these questions and the answers we learned from researchers such as Drs. Betty Hart and Todd Risely, and Dr. Pamela High, MD. We are grateful to those individuals who laid the groundwork necessary to raise our awareness of the importance of spoken words on language and literacy development in babies. No one has done more to advance the cause of reading to children than Jim Trelease through his tireless cross-country lectures and book, *The Read-Aloud Handbook*. We have been inspired by his example.

Without the thoughtful, kindly assistance of our brilliant agent, Stefanie Von Borstel of Full Circle Literary, this book would not have become a reality. We also thank her partner, Lilly Ghahremani for all her behind-the-scenes work. If it weren't for Michael Lennie, of Lennie Literary, we wouldn't have met Stefanie and Lilly. We are indebted to all the parents who supplied photos, agreed to be interviewed, and shared their children's book experiences with us. We're also indebted to the skilled photographic work of Linda Posnick and to the early editing help we received from the editor of our first book, Bob Rowland. We thank Caroline's long-time beloved friend, Irina Gronborg, well-known botanical artist, who generously ventured beyond plants to create our parent and baby drawings. Thanks also goes to Bob

Cushman who has given many hours of technical support as well as friendship.

Caroline is deeply grateful to her wonderful daughters-in-law, Kelli and Karen, for all their love and assistance, and to her sons, Peter Abraham and John Abraham, for their fun, upbeat encouragement and support; her brother, A. Myles Jackson, author, slam poet, and artist, who got us started with his generous writing and editing advice; and to her loving fiancé, Larry Gust for his support and enthusiasm for this project and keeping everything running smoothly in their active lives.

Barbara is thankful to her mother, Kate Murty, a former teacher, who has always encouraged Barbara to persevere and put one foot in front of the other; and to her husband, Fernando, who is an exceptionally dedicated father, who took over while Barbara spent long hours on weekends working on this book.

Introduction

To most parents of newborns, kindergarten seems a long way off. Five years can seem like an eternity when you're dealing with diapering, nurs-

ing, bathing, and laundry. Yet before you know it, the months quickly go by, and your precious little one will be walking, talking, going to preschool, and suddenly starting her first day of kindergarten. In those short five years—and especially the first two—even though you may not realize it, you will be the first and most important teacher your child will ever have.

In fact, your influence will determine whether or not your child succeeds in school. No schoolteacher has the power that parents have to insure academic success. What is this power? It's the power to give your baby the gift of words. That's right! Words! Short words, long words, common words, and uncommon words.

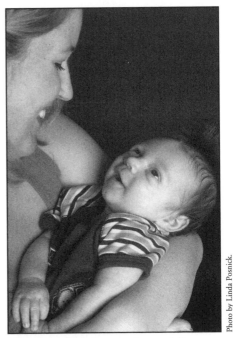

Mother cuddles her newborn while quietly speaking loving words.

Lots and lots of words everyday. Recent research tells us that what determines future academic success is the amount of words per hour babies hear before the age of two.[1]

As elementary school reading specialists, we see children who by the time they become of school age haven't heard enough words in their first years of life and thus lack the basic language building blocks necessary to learn how to read. Reading and writing skills begin at birth when baby is first exposed to language. Learning to read doesn't spontaneously happen when a child goes to school. It only comes easily when children have been immersed since birth in the world of words through a steady diet of hearing read-alouds and talk from their parents.

What is so magical about words that make such a difference in your baby's future? When you think about it, most communication and everything you learn in school involves words. Words are the basis of literacy, the ability to read and write. In order to succeed in school, children need to pay attention to, listen to, remember, understand, and speak words. These basic skills form the building blocks of literacy. Your baby acquires these building blocks naturally in the first years of life, but only if you set aside time every day to lovingly read and talk to your baby.

As caregivers you need to begin early, talking and reading with your babies before the age of two, while they are experiencing a critical period of brain growth and receptivity to language. Babies begin to start talking at around two. This means that from birth to two their brains have been absorbing the language in their environment at a pace and intensity that only happens in the first years of life. Although during the first couple days after birth your baby may be a little weary from the birth process, her brain is far more active than that of her parents. Her brain is working overtime preparing for her life's journey ahead. Parents play a critical role in this journey by supporting their baby's language and literacy development. However, just as babies need to be fed, loved, and nurtured, they need daily language nourishment to complete their brain development.

As you look at your peaceful, angelic newborn that only periodically opens her eyes to your loving gaze, you may ask whether reading to her can have any worthwhile effect. You might even feel silly reading when it appears there is no response. However, beneath your baby's seemingly passive demeanor is an active brain that is fed by the loving sounds of language, and its rhymes and playful noises. As early as six weeks, babies will respond by looking and listening intently and smiling. Before six weeks many of your baby's responses to your reading are invisible because they take place only in the brain. Even when baby is asleep the brain is busy making new brain cell connections in response to your reading aloud.

Babies come into the world with about 100 billion brain cells (neurons).[2]

It's what happens to those brain cells after birth that is crucial to brain development. After birth, a baby needs stimulation from the parents, and everyone and everything in his environment. That stimulation promotes new connections among brain cells that resemble a massive, wired communication system. At birth, there are few connections. But soon afterward, cells begin sprouting wiry antennae that are called axons and little receptors called dendrites. The axons transmit signals, and the dendrites receive information across a minute gap called a synapse, or connection. This activity accounts for the increases in brain and head size we observe as babies grow.[3] By the age of two, the number of brain connections escalates to 1 quadrillion (1,000 trillion).[4] That is roughly the number of stars in the universe.[5] As Emily Dickenson noted, "The brain is wider than the sky."[6]

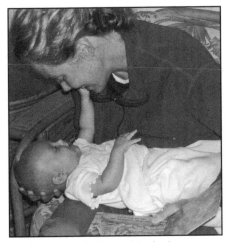

Every word you say and read to your baby creates a brain connection that results in your baby's brain growth.[7] Think of your words as baby brain food. Every time you read and reread a book, your baby's brain is absorbing information that will form his lifelong literacy foundation. This will lead to the thrilling milestones

Mother reads, talks, and lovingly interacts with her baby.

that you'll record in your journal, photographs, videos, and messages you tell your family and friends: your baby's first spoken words, your toddler's first full sentence, your child's first attempts to read, her successes at school, her graduations, and professional accomplishments. This is why reading aloud to your baby is the best investment you can make in your child's education.

The Purpose of This Book

Why did we, two elementary school reading specialists, write a book about the importance of reading to babies? Year in and year out we saw our beloved, bright-eyed kindergartners and first-graders come to us with little or no experience with books. In most cases we discovered that these eager students had almost never heard anyone read to them during their first five years of life.

As the read-aloud guru Jim Trelease states so simply, "If the child has never *heard* the word, the child will never *say* the word; and if you have neither heard it nor said it, it's pretty tough to *read* it and to *write* it."[8] We hope *Baby Read-Aloud Basics* will help parents discover it's fun and easy to read aloud to babies. Anyone can do it. All it takes are some books, and we tell you how to acquire the best for the least expense in Chapter 12. It's hard to imagine that anything so simple and easy can result in such critical benefits!

Baby Read-Aloud Basics offers a fun, interactive approach that gives parents both the information on the importance of read-alouds, and the guidance on how to read to babies. Parents will find reading aloud not only gives babies a sense of well-being, but also provides the underlying neurological nourishment for optimum language development and future academic success. It is our hope that *Baby Read-Aloud Basics* will help provide you with the information and know-how you need to develop a treasured daily read-aloud routine with your baby to give your little one the best possible start in life.

How This Book Is Organized

Baby Read-Aloud Basics is divided into three parts for easy and immediate use:

- *Part I: Shares WHY parents need to nourish their baby's brain with words.* You will learn about the most important benefits of reading to your baby, supported by recent studies that show how literacy begins at birth, and how the effects of reading aloud influence future reading and learning ability. The basics of reading aloud show how to get ready for your read-aloud routine.

- *Part II: Shows parents HOW to make the most of read-alouds starting at birth.* In an interactive format, six read-aloud stages include step-by-step instructions, read-aloud demonstrations, recommended book types, and a guide to recommended titles. Everything parents need to read with their babies starting from day one!

- *Part III: Gives resources, questions and answers, interviews, and practical tips.*
  Offers real-life success stories, resources, and answers to important issues facing today's busy parents, including how to manage television watching, how to read to baby when parents speak different languages, how to ensure that children build language skills with a nanny or caretaker, and where to find the time for read-alouds during busy days.

Reading aloud brings attachment, intimacy, and harmony between parent and baby. Although in this book we use "your baby," the person doing the read-alouds could be a grandparent, a loving caretaker, or any family member. When we use "mom," "mother," or "dad," we mean any personal caregiver who has a loving relationship with the baby. We use "he" and "she" in alternating chapters to honor both sexes.

Photo by Linda Posnick.

It is our hope that in the near future all students will come to school having been read to in the first five years of their lives, and that their bright eyes will light up with joy at the ease of becoming new readers. We hope that most reading difficulties will become a condition of the past, and that children will soon be saved from such suffering. All it takes is the commitment to get books and read-aloud know-how into every home, preschool, and childcare facility. Start reading to your child

Even at four months this baby is captivated by the illustrations in one of his favorite books.

today and make a difference in your child's life and in the world!

PART I

Why Baby Read-Alouds Benefit Your Baby's Language Development

CHAPTER 1

Ten Benefits of Reading Aloud to Your Baby from Day One

Let's take a look at ten ways your baby will benefit from a daily read-aloud routine. The emotional, mental, physical, and sensory benefits of daily reading to your baby are too great to ignore! Important research highlights the crucial role parents take in laying the building blocks that form their child's language and literacy foundation. Your baby's brain is equipped to absorb enormous amounts of information. Because of new technologies, we are witnesses to the incredible wonders of human infant development that begin well before birth. For example, new evidence tells us that seemingly passive babies are, in terms of brain activity, more active than adults. We now know that it is the time before babies start talking—from birth to two—that is critical for their future language development. This chapter will show you the benefits of reading to your baby—from enjoying calming moments together to starting the foundation of learning development and future academic success.

1. Read-Alouds Promote Listening Skills

Every language is different, and yet, babies all over the world quickly become experts in their own language. For example, in French you would say *le maison blanc,* or the house white. In English you would say *the white house*. How do babies learn the correct word order of their own languages? They learn by listening to their families.

Listening is a critical skill in the formation of language. Your baby has already begun listening to you since the last few months of pregnancy, and by birth has a fairly well developed hearing ability. Communication is a basic survival instinct for all life forms. Parents start talking to their baby before and after birth, beginning the interactive dialogue that will later turn into give-and-take conversations. Parents notice how intently newborns listen. Newborns instantly recognize their parents' voices and can already begin to recognize the difference between their parents' language and other languages. Within four months, babies not only know how the spoken language of their parents sounds, but recognize their own names.[1]

After hearing hundreds of books read aloud, by the time children go to school they can tell the difference between spoken language and the language of books. The language of books has its own style, and it is different from most spoken language. For example, in a book, if a verse form is used, it may have rhyming words, and a special rhythm. It may also have expressive nonsense words, like the following passage from Jane Yolen's *Off We Go!* (see Chapter 7):

> Scritch-Scratch, scritchity scratch,
> Directly from the egg I hatch,
> Then off to Grandma's house I dash,
> Sings Little Duck.[2]

We wouldn't typically use the above word order in everyday spoken language. Most of us might say something like, "I hatched directly from the egg, and I'm rushing to Grandma's house." The sooner babies are introduced to book language, the better. Books give additional practice in hearing the structure, grammar, and word order of language.

Some baby books have phrases, the basic elements of which are repeated on every page. For example, "Was Santa in the chimney? Was Santa near the Christmas tree? Was Santa in the kitchen?" And so on. This repetition of the question form using similar phrasing helps babies absorb a useful language pattern. Each baby or children's book has some element of language or a pattern, that when heard repeatedly, helps babies internalize book as well as spoken language. This repeated exposure gives children a head start once they go to school. It will allow them to comprehend more complex stories like chapter books and ease into the reading and writing process. The sooner babies are introduced to book language, the better.

When a child has the ability to listen attentively, he can easily absorb the thousands of words of vocabulary, sounds, and structure of language. By listening, he will eventually understand the meaning of what is being said. Soon he will begin speaking all those words he has heard from birth.

2. Read-Alouds Increase the Number of Vocabulary Words Babies Hear

Drs. Betty Hart and Todd Risley, in their book *Meaningful Differences in the Everyday Experience of Young American Children,* completed a comprehensive study that recorded the spoken language interactions between the children and parents from forty-two families who ranged from professional to low-income backgrounds. The researchers recorded the parent-child conversations for one hour each month over a period of two-and-a-half years. At age nine, the same children were retested for academic progress in school. The research demonstrates that what determines academically successful children is *the amount of language or talk they hear per hour from adults in the first few years of life.*[3] The study also shows that *the number of words babies hear each day is the single most important predictor of future intelligence, school success, and social skills.* Here are some of their significant findings about the language differences in children:

- Eleven-to-eighteen-month-old children from professional families heard an average of 2,150 words per hour. Working-class children heard an average of 1,250 words per hour, and low-income children heard only 620 words per hour.

- Professional mothers spoke to their babies using more complex language that included a variety of nouns, verbs, and adjectives, while low-income parents used fewer words and often used commands. Professional parents asked questions of their children, and followed their child's lead by talking about whatever the child said or babbled, thereby expanding the conversation. (See examples of this type of interaction in the demonstrations of parents reading to their babies in Chapters 3 to 8.)

- Children from professional families had lots of books in their bedrooms, an indication that they had access to books and were read to before bed.

- Babies from professional families heard a much higher frequency of positive feedback, while low-income family babies heard more negative feedback. (See examples of positive feedback in the demonstrations of parents reading to their babies in Chapters 3 to 8.)

- By age two, a child from a professional family would have heard about 24 million cumulative words from their families. Working-class children would have heard about 15 million words, and low-income children only about 8 million. By age four this number escalated to 45 million for professional family children, 26 million for working-class children, and 13 million for low-income children. This means that by age four, professional family children heard 32 million more words than the low-income family children in the study. By the time these children entered kindergarten there was even more of a word gap.

- The children in the study were tested again at age three, and testing showed that the number and quality of words the three-year-old children heard when they were babies predicted the number of words in their spoken vocabularies when they were ages three and nine. It also predicted their IQs (100 is average): 117 for the children of professional families, 107 for children of working class families, and 79 for the low-income children. By the time the children reached nine years of age, the testing scores reflected the same gaps. The children who heard the fewest words had not caught up to those who heard an abundance of words before ages two and three.

This study demonstrates the significant role parents play in providing the quality and quantity of language necessary for their child's academic success. All the families in the study loved and cared for their children. The low-income families didn't know how to communicate with their babies in a way that generated a rich abundance of ongoing conversation that was predominately positive and full of words. There is hope, however, for helping families learn how to give their children more vocabulary, as you'll see in the research of Dr. Pamela High later in this chapter.

3. Read-Alouds Develop Attention Span and Memory

In recent years, schoolteachers have noticed that there is an increasing number of children who cannot pay attention for any length of time when in school. One study links this trend to the increased time that children watch television and other screen media (see Chapter 10). Children who are read to on a daily basis are known to have long attention spans. You'll notice how long your two- and three-month-old can hold his interest in the give-and-take dialogue that takes place during a reading session (see Chapter 2 on parentese).

The abilities to pay attention and remember are related. How can you remember something when you don't give it your full attention? When you read aloud to your baby day in and day out, you are repeating various words and phrases, describing, and talking about illustrations. Babies are capable of an intense concentration that you don't see in older children. Their brains are searching and scanning everything they come in contact with in order to get information and meaning. If this ability to pay attention is not nurtured from day one, we are teaching our babies just the opposite: to have divided attention. Watching television teaches children to get information in short, fast, scattered visual and sound bits and pieces. Reading, on the other hand, requires a thoughtful presence of mind extended over a longer period.

Reading aloud to your baby is the best way to help develop attention and memory. Babies learn how to focus their attention in a quiet atmosphere, listen to your voice, remember what they hear, and respond using body language, coos, and babbles until they can answer using their own words. If read to on a regular basis using the suggested "parentese" voice methods outlined in Chapter 2, some babies can hold their attention steadily for at least a half hour. By around age eighteen months to two years, your baby will be able to remember all the words in a book after only a few readings. By around two or three years, your baby will remember language patterns in nursery rhymes and books. No matter what age, they will be fascinated by the tones of your voice, the sounds of your language, and the captivating, colorful illustrations. What a beautiful way to bring up your child resonating to the harmony, peace, and joy imparted in children's books. No wonder your child wants to keep his attention focused during the time you are reading aloud. No wonder he'll eventually memorize some of the passages and refrains you've read to him.

4. Read-Alouds Help Babies Learn Uncommon Words

When you read to your baby, he hears both your words and the words from the book. Words from children's books are different and more unusual than everyday conversational words. A study by Donald P. Hayes and Margaret G. Ahrens shows that everyday conversational language is rather simple and straightforward.[4] Its main purpose is to make the point quickly, whether adults are talking to each other or to children. The pitch, rhythm, pace, and volume may change when talking to babies (see Chapter 2 for description of "parentese"), but the complexity of the speaking vocabulary remains relatively low.

This eight-month-old can focus her attention for long periods because she is accustomed to having family members like grandma read to her daily.

According to the Hayes-Ahrens study, there are 5,000 words that are used commonly in everyday language. In addition, there are 5,000 more everyday words that are used less frequently. Together they form the basic 10,000 commonly used words. Any words not in this lexicon are called "rare words." Words were given a rank according to their frequency of use in written language. For example, "the" is the most used word and is ranked number 1. Any word that is ranked higher than 10,000 would be considered rare. For example, the frequency rate of "amplifier" is ranked at 16,000. The study shows that most spoken language occurs in the 400–600 range, which is quite low.[5]

How do children learn rare words if they don't ordinarily hear them spoken? They learn them from hearing books read aloud or from reading. Even baby books, according to the study, have 16.3 rare words per thousand, compared to 9.3 rare words per thousand when adults speak to children. It's the rare words that children need to learn in order to be able to understand story books read to them in school or books and textbooks they will read to gain knowledge and information.[6] The following charts show the amounts of rare words per thousand in conversation and in print.[7]

NUMBER OF RARE WORDS PER THOUSAND: IN CONVERSATION	
Adults talking to infants 0–2 years	9.3
Adults talking to preschool children 2–5 years	9.0
Adults talking to school-age children 6–12 years	11.7
Adults talking to adults	17.3

NUMBER OF RARE WORDS PER THOUSAND: IN PRINT	
Preschool books	16.3
Children's books	30.9
Comic books	53.5
Adult books	52.7
Popular magazines	65.7
Newspapers	68.3
Scientific articles	128.0

NUMBER OF RARE WORDS PER THOUSAND: CONVERSATION AND PRINT	
Adults talking to infants 0–2 years	9.3
Preschool books	16.3
Children's books	30.9

We have seen from the Hart-Risley study and in our own classrooms that many children don't even have a sufficient number of the basic 5,000 words in their vocabulary. To excel in school, in the marketplace, and in life, every child needs access to the full range of commonly spoken words as well as the more uncommon written vocabulary of books. According to the Hart-Risley study, all parents regardless of socioeconomic level tend to speak less to their children during the time before two years of age when children need to hear the most language. Not only does your child need lots of everyday language before two, but lots of language that includes more uncommon words, the words found in children's books. If babies hear some rare words everyday, these words will eventually become part of the vocabulary they understand as well as their spoken vocabulary.

Examples of Uncommon Words Your Baby Hears When You Read to Her

What are examples of uncommon or rare words that you are likely to see on the printed page but not hear in typical conversation? Following is a selection of some uncommon words from infant board books that appear in the Baby Book Reviews at-a-Glance at the end of Chapters 3 to 8. We don't know whether every one of these words is officially rare, or above the 10,000th in rank. We do know that preschool or baby books have 16.3 rare words per thousand compared to an average of 9.3 rare words per thousand used in spoken language to babies up to two years of age. So we can assume that most baby books you read to your baby will have at least one or more rare words.

Each of the fun words below inspires the imagination. Yet we probably wouldn't use most of these words in our daily talk with babies or other family members. Words like *slither, collide, fluffy,* and *darkness* conjure up a magical world that brings joy and wonder to the ears of babies and toddlers. Not that a child might not hear these words occasionally in conversation, but it's the context of the stories in which they occur and the repetition of the telling of the stories that expands a baby's brain connections and reinforces neural (brain cell) pathways. This reinforcement allows babies to quickly retrieve these words when needed in future conversation, reading, or writing.

A SELECTION OF UNCOMMON AND PERHAPS RARE WORDS FROM INFANT BOARD BOOKS IN CHAPTERS 3 TO 8			
young	darkness	paddled	frightened
fetch	struck	fiddle	twirl
bounce	spin	prance	skitter
swing	scramble	swirl	meadow
slime	creep	slither	dash
aircraft	passenger	steep	tow
collide	quilted	parasol	darkness
daylight	furious	giggling	extinguish
enormous	excitement	quarreling	grinning
fluffy	peek	darting	flashy
flipping	scales	stripes	spotted
flamingo	walrus	whale	zebra

As our examples of parents reading to their babies in Chapters 3 to 8 demonstrate, the amount of talk and conversation escalates when reading a book. In addition to the words read from the book's pages, the book actually provides a vehicle for much more conversation than usual between parent and child—which is another plus of reading aloud to babies. Often this conversation includes some of the book's uncommon or rare words.

When toddlers begin to talk, they *understand* far more words than they can initially speak. When children begin learning to read around school age, they *understand* many more words than they can actually read. Preschool- and kindergarten-age children need to comprehend the many directions and discussions taking place in their classrooms. They will need to comprehend the stories heard during read-aloud time. As they begin to learn to read, rare words will not be problematic if they have heard their parents read and talk about these words (as well as hundreds and hundreds of others) from birth.

In the following selection of words from a typical first-grade textbook, you'll see words that you normally don't use in everyday conversation, yet are necessary for a child to understand in order to have good reading comprehension. In our experience as reading specialists, these and hundreds of other uncommon or rare words are those that struggling readers unfortunately do not understand. In most cases, the students with low vocabularies have not been read to on a regular basis, have watched too much television, and have not been involved in enough adult-to-child conversation.

A SELECTION OF WORDS FROM A FIRST-GRADE READING TEXTBOOK[8]				
greedy	crew	slinky	equal	argued
appetite	stalked	flicked	fraction	half
field	meadow	canoe	delighted	expected
appear	gather	journey	pleasant	creep

5. Read-Alouds Help Babies Learn to Understand the Meanings of Words

Kindergartners come to school with incredible differences in vocabulary development. Children learn vocabulary in the home from birth to five from hearing their parents, caregivers, and other adults talk and read to them. The amount of vocabulary children understand by the time they get to kindergarten determines how well they will achieve academically. Almost all the teaching for the first two years of school is oral, including listening to books read aloud by the teacher. How well children understand what is read aloud and spoken to them determines how well they will learn to read and comprehend what they read. Children who have difficulties understanding oral language in the classroom are sometimes identified as having auditory processing problems that require the services of a speech and language pathologist.

Understanding vocabulary is the basis of communication, literacy, and intelligence. The only way babies and toddlers can learn and understand vocabulary is to hear words directly from a person who is talking to them. Television and radio cannot teach babies vocabulary.[9] The American Academy of Pediatrics is quite specific in their recommendation that children under two should not watch television.[10] Babies like to hear talk directly from their parents or caregivers. Parents naturally speak in what is called "parentese" or "motherese" (see Chapter 2), and this sing-songy, child-directed speech with its long, drawn-out vowel sounds and comforting tones

Typical kindergarten classroom where children are expected to sit, listen, and comprehend a story.

encourages language development and makes conversation meaningful to babies.

What is the most important skill of good readers? Many parents might say the answer to this question is phonics. Why? Because it would seem that when you know the sounds of the letters in the alphabet, you could sound out and read any word. But sounding out words isn't enough. Without a large vocabulary and an understanding of what you're reading, you're not really reading, just saying a blend of sounds. In addition, some words with which you are unfamiliar may defy proper sounding out. When you already know the word's meaning it's easy to sound it out, but what good does it do to sound out every word if you don't understand what the words are communicating?

Comprehension is the most important skill of good readers. The whole purpose of reading and writing is to communicate information. This ability begins developing at birth when your baby listens intently to gain meaning from your words, tone of voice, facial expressions, and actions. To read is to understand the messages in all those black symbols on a white page. Before a child can understand the symbols, he has to understand the spoken word. Listening comprehension leads to reading comprehension.

Recent research conducted under the direction of Pamela High, M.D., through the Department of Pediatrics at Rhode Island Hospital, proves that children from any income group can achieve enhanced language development when families receive developmentally appropriate children's books, educational materials, and advice about sharing books with babies and toddlers.[11]

The study was conducted with a multicultural group of 205 low-income families with five- to eleven-month-old babies. About half of the families (106) were given books, materials, and personal instructions on how to read books daily to their babies. The parents and children usually read together at bedtime. The other 99 parents in the control group were given no books or instruction in how to use them. All the 205 families were visited three or four times by the researchers. When the children in the study were revisited at eighteen months, 75 percent were given receptive vocabulary (the vocabulary that toddlers understand, but cannot yet say) tests. The testing showed the following results:

- There was a 40 percent increase in receptive vocabulary (words babies understand, but may not yet speak) in the children whose parents received books and personal instructions on how to use them. The children whose families received no books or instructions had only a 16 percent increase in receptive vocabulary.

- The families who received books and personal instructions read more with their toddlers.

- Parents who received books and personal instructions said they changed their attitudes toward the importance of reading with infants and toddlers.

- Parents who read to their babies and toddlers said reading aloud was one of their child's favorite activities, and one of parents' favorite activities to do with their child.

This promising research shows that any parent can give their child all the language advantages that daily reading aloud provides. All they need is the encouragement, the books, and the know-how. More importantly, this research demonstrates that reading aloud to babies achieves an increase in receptive vocabulary that will later translate into spoken vocabulary and the skills necessary for reading and writing.

6. Read-Alouds Help Babies Learn Concepts About Print

In kindergarten and even first grade, some children can't distinguish between a word, letter, or number. These concepts along with other knowledge about books, such as recognizing the front cover with the title, are tested in kindergarten with the CAP (*Concepts About Print*) test.[12] Children who have been read to since birth will easily know these concepts. By preschool many children can identify letters, numbers, and perhaps a few words. But even if they don't know what the words, letters, or numbers say, they know the difference, and can point to a number in response to the prompt, "Point to the number."

Repeated readings of counting books like Molly Bang's *Ten, Nine, Eight* will expose babies and toddlers to numbers. After the age of two, your toddler will have seen hundreds of books with numbers, words, and letters of different sizes and fonts. (See Chapters 3 to 8 for all the books mentioned here.)

Another concept babies learn when they are read to is that we read from left to right and from top to bottom. After watching their parent's finger sweep across the page under the print from left to right, babies internalize this movement, and their eyes automatically move in this direction too. A very small number of three-year-olds start reading after seeing their parents read to them like this on a daily basis. No matter when your child learns to read, his eyes will soon be trained in this left to right movement from the many times he followed his parent's finger sliding under the print. He also learns from the early age of around ten months to turn the pages in the right direction.

Understanding that they are supposed to get a message or meaning from print is a critical concept for toddlers to absorb once they begin to understand the meaning of words, sentences, and longer passages. Around eighteen months, when parents start pointing to the words they're reading, babies realize that many of the words coming out of daddy and mommy's mouths come from those black squiggly lines on the pages of his books. Babies soon learn that the print on the page carries a message. The whole point of reading is to gain meaning and understanding. When children understand the message of what they hear read to them, they will easily comprehend the message when they later become independent readers.

7. Read-Alouds Help Babies Learn to Get Information from Illustrations

Illustrations are almost as important as the text in baby books when it comes to generating language and inspiring the imagination. The reason the words in books are so important is that they include rare words that you usually don't use in regular conversation. However, the illustrations or photographs are helpful in stimulating baby's visual development. As baby's binocular vision grows along with the ability to notice details, book illustrations can aid visual development.

The best thing about the illustrations is that they encourage conversation. In fact, in some cases, you don't even have to read the text, or there is no text. You "read" the pictures. Such is the case with Tana Hoban's *White on Black*, a wordless picture book, or the almost wordless *Carl's Afternoon in the Park* by Alexandra Day. After a few months of being read to since birth, babies can tell the difference when you're reading and when you're talking about the pictures. You may point to certain words for emphasis, like "no" in *No, David!* by David Shannon. Other times you'll point to the illustration of the tiny mouse in *Goodnight Moon* by Margaret Wise Brown or the colorful keys in *Good Night, Gorilla* by Peggy Rathmann. Your baby will see you point to words and illustrations over and over and understand the different kinds of information you get from each.

Sometimes, especially when your baby is beginning to understand more and more words after about nine months, you may look at a book like

Photo by Linda Posnick.

This three-month-old is attempting to focus on the colorful illustrations of a book mom is reading to him.

Richard Scarry's *Best First Book Ever!*, point to the illustrations, and label them: ball, shoes, pajamas. There are a variety of illustrated books with or without labels. The wordless picture book *White on Black,* though simple with one image on each page, is one of the first books babies see when they're introduced to labeling at two months (see Chapter 4).

Not that you expect two-month-old babies to know what you are talking about, but their vision and hearing is being stimulated, as you comfort them with words and attention. You are introducing them to the process of reading pictures and having a conversation. Soon this process will be second nature, and they will know all about getting information from illustrations. At about nine or ten months (if you have read to him daily since birth), your baby will crawl over to the bookshelf or book box, take out his favorite book, and independently look at the pictures and turn the pages. Usually, only babies who have been read to daily from birth can do this independently.

8. Read-Alouds Promote Bonding and Calmness for Both Baby and Parent

Photo by Linda Posnick.

Most parents who read regularly to their babies say they love it. We often hear: "I look forward to our special reading time" or "It's so relaxing." Reading aloud is one of the easiest and least complicated of all the daily tasks that you do with your baby. It helps you bond and attach to your baby because you're putting everything aside to give full attention to your precious little one. It promotes family togetherness. It's a built-in (routine) time-out for you, as well as for your children. It's as essential for baby's emotional and mental development as food is for physical development.

This father and his baby have already bonded through their daily reading routine.

Children's books, with their adorable illustrations, are usually so magical that they weave their calming spell over you and your baby. A new mother might be tired from the changes a newborn brings to the family routine. Taking time to sit and gaze at your baby while he listens to a little story, even for a few minutes, is calming. It's good for both you and your baby, especially when you know you are providing your child essential nutrients for his brain. This routine will bring bonding and closeness for many years to come.

For dads, read-alouds can be an important way to immediately bond with baby and continue this important relationship right through the early school years. Right after birth, mom is still physically bonding with baby through nursing. By reading to baby, dad is fulfilling the important role of feeding baby's brain with words. In this way, dad will also feel attached to baby, and little by little this relationship will become routine, a habit that baby loves and comes to expect. What better way for dads to bond with their newborn!

9. Read-Alouds Stimulate the Imagination and All the Senses

Teachers notice that children who watched several hours of television a day when they were babies and preschoolers show less creativity and imagination. Listening to a storyteller or a story from a book that is dramatized, whether fiction or nonfiction, helps children learn to form images in their heads using sensual memories like how things feel, taste, smell, sound, or look. This process helps children make sense out of what they hear and leads to good reading comprehension. It causes them to think, to wonder, to perceive using their senses, and to empathize—important ingredients in living a rewarding, thoughtful, and happy life. Imagination leads to psychological and spiritual health.

All great cultural, artistic, scientific, and philosophical contributions come about because of the ideas generated by our imaginations. The word *imagination* comes from *image*, the ability to use our senses to form images with our inner vision. Most thinking involves imagery. Imagination is the key to play, which is so important to children's development. Yet as teachers, we see a number of children who cannot pretend. These children often have less vocabulary and have watched too much television. Imagination allows us to imagine our future and plan what we will do with our lives.

When you see a particularly animated parent or grandparent reading to a baby, you notice how, in addition to dramatizing the words, they point to the illustrations and direct baby's eyes to a particular object like an orange. They may say something like, "This is what an orange looks like. Can you imagine what it smells like, what it feels like? Let's get a real orange and see." Then baby can touch the orange and smell it. He looks at it and is told this is what orange, the color, and orange, the fruit, looks like, and so on. Then the orange is broken apart in order to further smell the peel, then lick and taste the inside sweet, juicy pulp. All this touching, smelling, seeing, hearing, and tasting stimulates brain cells and is recorded for future reference.

There are endless opportunities for sensual exploration during read-alouds! As many of the senses as possible should be brought into play when reading. This helps babies strengthen their senses of touch, smell, hearing, visual, and taste perceptions, all of which support the eventual reading process.

10. Read-Alouds Instill the Love of Books and Learning

When a nine- or ten-month-old independently goes to pull out his books from his bookshelf, he does so because he has experienced that books give pleasure even when he just sits for a short time by himself and looks at them. That independent pleasure is associated with the pleasure he gets cuddling with his parents and reading before naps or bedtime. The association of books with love and comfort will last a lifetime. The joy of reading will serve him well in school where studies show that students who read for pleasure outside of school are the high achievers.

Enjoying reading is an important part of the literacy equation because it involves the emotions and the motivation to read. Without the motivation to read, children don't read. As children progress through school, the amount of reading for pleasure accomplished outside of school adds hundreds of words to their vocabulary, many of which are rare words. One study shows that during a typical school year children at the 90th percentile (the top of their class) read 200 times more words outside of school than children at the 10th percentile of their classes.[13] Not only does all this reading enlarge vocabulary, it literally expands the brain through the multiplication of brain connections and neural pathways, so important for thinking skills and achievements of all kinds.

When you read to your baby, you are giving your child some of life's greatest gifts: the cuddly, loving warmth of a close, one-to-one daily read-

This nine-month-old enjoys looking at the books her parents have read to her.

aloud time, an enriched vocabulary that forever expands the mind, a knowledge of everything about books and all that can be learned from them, and a motivation and love of reading that will lead to a happy, successful life. How wonderful that the simple act of daily read-alouds reaps so many benefits for babies. You don't have to be super mom or dad. You don't need special qualifications. All you need is books. With books, any parent no matter what educational background or culture can be their child's most important and beloved teacher. So start reading to your baby today!

CHAPTER 2

Eight Baby Read-Aloud Basics

What You Need to Know to Get Started

Now that you've read in Chapter 1 about the wide-reaching benefits of reading to your baby, you probably can't wait to get started. Just look over the following eight baby read-aloud basics, and you and your baby can begin a journey together that will enrich your lives. Besides the calming and bonding benefits, you'll develop a conversational resonance through everyday ideas and events that children's books inspire. In the very beginning you may feel like it's a one-way monologue, but before you know it, you'll be in a dialogue in which your baby responds to you by locking her eyes in rapt attention on your eyes, your mouth, and the book. She'll wiggle her legs and arms, and breathe faster. In return you'll read more to her, and the read-aloud dance is underway with all its lifetime benefits of increased vocabulary and language skills.

1. Newborns Need a Quiet Reading Environment

As your baby makes the transition from a uterine environment to our noisy, well-lit, open-air world, many physiological changes are taking place. A newborn's perceptual system does not screen out everything that her eyes see, her ears hear, or her skin feels. Be sensitive to your newborn's needs by providing quiet time when she can listen clearly to your voice as you talk or read to her. When reading to your baby, turn off any competing noises, such as the television, stereo, or radio. In early infancy, it is especially important to prevent overstimulation or stress. During read-alouds, allow your baby to hear only your rhythmic voice without the disturbance of background noises.

2. Newborns Are Comforted by the Sound of Your Voice

Initially, right after your child's birth, you have a lot of leeway in what you may select to read to your baby. One parent told us he read aloud from the stock market pages of the newspaper. Since babies are mostly focusing on your voice at the outset, you could read anything aloud. However, since babies love your melodious voice, the best choice right after birth might be any kind of rhymes, such as "Mother Goose." Some parents start right out with board books, such as *Goodnight Moon,* and note that their babies become so accustomed to these books that they continue to request them for the first year or longer. Gradually you will become aware of your baby's favorites and select books that you know she would like. As babies mature, they become pickier and let you know what they like through their body language. Whatever you choose to read, become aware of the effect of the sound of your voice on your baby. Note your baby's excited movements when you read with enthusiasm or change the pitch of your voice.

3. Hold and Cuddle Your Baby When You Read

The most important thing to remember when reading a book to your infant is that you are providing love, attention, and intimacy while giving important language input. When babies are old enough to begin to choose books and bring them to you to read, often what they really want is to cuddle and to be given loving attention.

When you first hold a newborn it can feel awkward, especially before they can hold their heads up. Imagine holding a book and a newborn at the same time. After a little practice, you'll find the most comfortable position, whether it's in your favorite rocker with a "boppy" (a donut-shaped nursing pillow) or lying next to your baby on the bed.

4. When Choosing a Book, Allow Your Baby to Be Your Guide

There is no prescription from pediatricians, educators, or psychologists recommending a list of books for each stage of a child's early development.

This is a good thing, as we have never encountered identical lists of books from parents we interviewed. Each child is unique and has his own preferences. One size does not fit all. Parents begin early with books they think their child will like (see Chapters 3 to 8 for suggested books) and then reread many, many times those that get a favorable reaction. Newborns benefit most from hearing your familiar voice reading poems or books with rhythm and rhyme when they are awake or asleep. After the first two or three months, your baby will react favorably by looking back and forth with interest between your face and the book, wiggling her legs and hands with excitement, or smiling happily. Conversely, if your baby is not enthused about a book she may look away from your face and the book, push the book aside, or fall asleep. By the time your baby is a year or more, she will select the books she wants you to read from the shelf, pile, or basket.

Your choice of books is not as important as making the choice to read to your baby on a regular basis. By making that choice, you will give your baby a powerful boost of language development, the benefits of which will last a lifetime. More importantly, your baby will associate reading with cuddly love and attention.

5. Start Reading at Any Page

You don't have to finish a book, or even start at the beginning. You can go right to the part you know your baby likes best and have fun on one or more pages by dramatizing different parts with a variety of voice inflections and tones. Your baby may even want to switch back and forth between one book and another. Often baby books do not contain stories, but illustrated rhymes or labeled pictures. Skipping around the text is easy in these types of books. If there is a story line, it still doesn't matter if you pick and choose pages that interest your baby.

6. You Don't Have to Read All of the Words in the Book

Sometimes you'll find that your baby prefers that you merely point to the illustrations and name some objects, or that you make up your own words or story as you go along rather than reading what the words on the page say. Your baby will let you know. For example, when you select a favorite book for your baby, if you know from previous readings that your child prefers a certain page, you can turn directly to that page. You can read it in the way your baby loves to hear, perhaps dramatizing certain sentences or words by speaking them more loudly or in a squeaky voice. How will you know what pages your baby likes best? She may wiggle her arms and legs or gaze at the page with great interest. She might also look at the page longer than other pages.

For a wordless picture book, like Tana Hoban's *White on Black,* you may dream up anything you want to say about the pictures of simple objects. Your baby will show you which pictures she's most intrigued by. In this interaction with your baby the most important element is listening, observing and following your baby's cues. Your baby will let you know what pages she prefers and how long to remain on a page. Usually, at this stage it's best to remain on a page for only a few seconds.

7. Repeated Readings Are Good for Baby's Language Development

As soon as your child can speak in phrases some of the first words you'll hear are "read it again." Hearing language from books repeatedly helps children memorize it. Eight-month-olds can remember certain words that are read to them after two weeks of hearing repeated readings.[1] Reading the same books over and over again may seem an interminable task, but the language benefits as well as your child's joy will keep you going. Even at birth babies have been shown to prefer hearing books that were read to them in utero. Researchers gave newborns a choice between hearing their mothers read a new book or hearing a book read repeatedly before birth. Using a sucking device, babies responded by increased sucking when they heard the familiar book read to them before birth.[2] (See Chapter 3 for examples of parents who read to their babies before birth.) Rereading of traditional nursery rhymes starting at birth helps your baby identify and learn the sounds of his language. A good knowledge of sound discrimination forms the basis of later reading and writing skills.

8. Use "Parentese" When Reading and Talking to Your Baby

If you think reading to babies is having a quiet baby on your lap soaking up every word that you read straight from the book, think again. Reading to babies looks and feels very different from reading to older children. The principal difference in reading to babies as opposed to older children is the way you interrelate using your voice and a baby book. This way of talking to newborns is called *parentese*. When parents are in intimate face-to-face contact with their babies, they speak in a singsongy, higher pitched, slower, louder voice. When reading, you'll use the baby book primarily as a vehicle to converse and dialogue with your baby using your parentese voice. As we mentioned previously, you may use none, some, or all of the words in the book to have this kind of conversation.

Studies show that beginning at around five weeks, babies prefer parentese, rather than regular adult conversation.[3] Parentese is the best way for babies to hear and learn language. Studies show that it takes babies twice as long as adults to process information.[4] With parentese you speak more slowly so babies can hear the individual sounds and words in the stream of speech. This helps them distinguish the unique rhythm of the language spoken in the home. Babies learn language best when parents speak with their parentese voices using face-to-face, personal, baby-directed talk. The more parentese talk babies hear before the age of two, the more words they'll learn. A large vocabulary will lead to higher intelligence and academic achievement in school. Parentese aids in the process of learning the sounds, grammar, and structure of language, necessary for effective speaking, reading, and writing.

Main Features of Parentese[5]

When speaking or reading to their babies, parents:

- Put their faces very close to the baby's face
- Use shorter utterances
- Speak in a melodious tone
- Articulate clearly
- Vary and raise their pitch
- Frequently use repetition
- Use exaggerated facial expressions (eye contact, raising of eyebrows, and big smiles)
- Move their bodies rhythmically
- Lengthen vowels (soooooo cuuuuuute)
- Use shorter sentences
- Use longer pauses

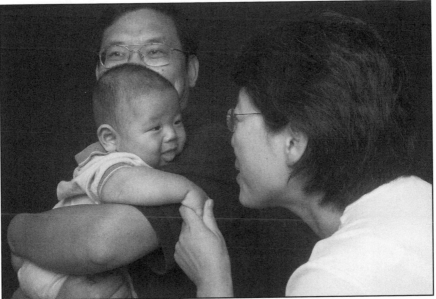

Photo by Linda Posnick.

Parents all over the world speak an intimate form of baby-directed talk, called parentese.

- Put unfamiliar words at the ends of sentences for stress ("Gavin, look over there at the *bulldozer!*")
- Give positive feedback and loving attention (in response to a babble, "That's right, look at all those flowers!"). See demonstrations of parents reading to their babies in Chapters 4 to 9.

What Is the Difference Between Parentese and Baby Talk?

Parentese is not baby talk, though what some people mean by baby talk is actually parentese. Baby talk is the actual altering of the spelling of the words to utterances bordering on nonsense. It can turn a sentence like, "Look at the cute little baby" into "Wook at zu coot wittle babykins." It is very distorted and would actually delay infant language development if that is what babies usually heard.

Some parents might even feel uncomfortable speaking parentese, because they are not used to using it, or they may think their newborns can't understand, so why bother? Newborns can't yet understand. Babies need exposure to language from day one to eventually understand. But first they need to be immersed in words to hear the tone and rhythm of their language. Listening in the first few months of life is a key building block in the formation of good language. Parentese helps babies hear and learn their parent's language. Parents will find that speaking parentese is part of the natural bonding process. In fact, many parents may not even realize they are using their voice in this new way.

How Does the Use of Parentese Change from Infancy to Age Two?

Along with *parentese*, the other two main features of reading to babies are *dialogue* (or conversing with babies) and *questioning*. For newborns, dialogue occurs when they respond to read-alouds by moving their hands or feet, cooing, breathing faster, or giving you some bodily signal of response and pleasure. After you talk and read a little, allow your baby time to respond in some of these ways. Then respond to her by talking some more. For example, when your baby starts moving her arms or legs as you read and look at a page with a bright yellow duck, you might say in your singsongy voice, "You like that page because it's about that cute little yellow duck like the one you have." Dialoguing in this way feels natural. Trying to read the book straight through without responding to your baby feels unnatural. Try it both ways, and you'll see for yourself. You're teaching your baby the turn taking of communication while giving her a constant stream of words, so necessary for language development. It's also so much more; it's an intimate bonding through words that uniquely happens in the act of reading, talking, and cuddling.

The books parents select and the way they read them will change from the baby's birth to age two. For example, the book that you read to your baby in infancy will be read differently at eighteen months. At birth, parents will read in a more rhythmic way with fewer interruptions that gives the sense of the flow of the language. This is why parents traditionally read nursery rhymes to new babies. As baby's vision develops between two and four months, parents can use their parentese voice to direct baby's attention to books that have brightly colored illustrations. When babies start cooing and babbling, your parentese will include uttering and dramatizing the sounds in baby's environment like trains (choo, choo) or animals (wuff, wuff), for example.

At about three months, parents begin asking questions (see demonstrations of parents reading to their babies in Chapters 3 to 8). Questioning is good for babies because it is a direct verbal link to your baby, and helps you connect with his needs. As baby develops, it keeps her attention, and pulls her into the dialogue, especially before she can verbally respond. Later it helps toddlers develop problem-solving skills and encourages them to think and to ponder.

When your baby is around a year old, you'll start emphasizing the meaning of vocabulary words in books that are part of baby's daily experiences. As she becomes more social, you will use books to teach daily social interaction phrases, such as "thank you," "hello," and "goodbye." Your parentese will also include hand and facial gestures. You will be talking as much as reading when reading books that correspond to baby's experiences, such as going to the zoo, or looking at cars and trucks.

Read-aloud routines include time for cuddling and closeness.

As your baby turns into an independent toddler, your parentese will include repeated readings of books that require you to creatively animate the story in new ways. For example, you may find yourself on the floor slithering like a snake or hopping like a kangaroo! Your toddler will now be able to mimic many of your gestures, as well as invent some of her own. She can verbally give one- or two-word answers to your questions about locating different animals or objects in books. By reading hundreds of books over the first two years using your animated parentese voice, your toddler understands many more words than she can presently say. She has most of the prerequisites to becoming a successful reader.

You don't have to incorporate all of the above basics to begin. You'll find that you naturally read to your baby using many of the above principles such as intimately cuddling your baby and practicing parentese. As you become more experienced reading to your baby, you can gradually include more of the principles, ideas, and tips presented here and in Parts II and III of *Baby Read-Aloud Basics*. The read-aloud journey with your baby will bring hundreds of hours of enjoyment and benefits for many years to come. So don't let another day go by without reading to your baby!

PART II

The Six Baby Read-Aloud Stages

We have divided the ages from birth to two into six stages, based on language and physical development. The following "Six Baby Read-Aloud Stages" chart will help you see how your baby's relationship to books will change over time. Each of the six stages can be characterized by the name given to the stage. The names of the six stages reveal at a glance your baby's developmental journey toward becoming a talker, and eventually a reader: the Listener, the Observer, the Cooer, the Babbler, the Word Maker, and the Phrase Maker. Each stage on the chart lists the types of books parents may consider for reading aloud. Having this chart available at the library or bookstore will help you choose books that match the developmental characteristics of your baby.

Chapters 3 to 8 correspond to each stage, and give parents specific guidance on how to read to their babies. These chapters provide parents with the following information:

- Introduction to the stage
- Language and physical milestones: listening, verbal, visual, motor
- Step-by-step read-aloud instructions: how to position baby, parentese, challenges
- Read-aloud demonstration of a parent reading to baby
- What to notice in the read-aloud demonstration
- Types of books for the stage
- Baby book reviews at a glance—with parentese tips and illustration talking points

Six Baby Read-Aloud Stages: From Birth to Two

	Months	Language and Physical Characteristics of Baby[1]	Types of Books to Read
Stage 1 **The Listener** Chapter 3	0–2	• Is more responsive to rhymes and stories heard before birth. • Recognizes mother's voice and prefers it to other adult voices.	• Books with nursery rhymes • Books/rhymes read before birth • Anything for the purpose of baby hearing your comforting voice
Stage 2 **The Observer** Chapter 4	2–4	• Responds more positively to "parentese" (see Chapter 2) than regular speech tone. • Begins to synchronize movements of eyes and seek out certain features of the environment, such as mobiles, checkerboard patterns, and bright, contrasting colors.	• Books with rhymes and songs • Bold color or black-and-white picture books
Stage 3 **The Cooer** Chapter 5	4–8	• Recognizes own name at four months. • Can distinguish between the happy, sad, or angry tones of a parent's voice. • Can tell the difference between the language spoken at home and other languages. • Absorbs and memorizes large numbers of sounds and words that will form the foundation of later speech.	• Homemade books about baby with family and friends • Books that stimulate senses, touch-and-feel books • Teething books • Books with illustrations that are engaging and well matched to the text

- At six or seven months begins to make sounds that resemble real language—mamama, dadada.
- Can see colors and details clearly.
- Likes to examine different features and textures of objects with hands and mouth.

- Books containing words and pictures about daily routines, such as bathing, eating, and sleeping
- Books that label objects, toys, and parts of the body.
- Stage 2 books

***Stage 4
The Babbler***

Chapter 6

8–12

- Understands (but cannot yet say) an average of fifty words at twelve months.
- Is developing ability to remember language that is heard repetitively from books or routines with parents.
- Can say most speech sounds.
- Is beginning to make words at 10 months but will continue to babble beyond first year.
- Dialogues by gesturing, pointing, and verbalizing.
- Makes animal sounds instead of saying the animal name.
- Has fully developed color, detail, and depth perception.
- Has increasing control of hand movements. Will turn pages and point to pictures as you read.

- Homemade books about baby's first birthday
- Books that encourage toddlers to chime in and repeat a word or phrase
- Word books that label objects, toys, and parts of body
- Books that explore concepts, such as inside, outside, under, after, next
- Books that illustrate action words, such as running and jumping
- Books with flaps and noise buttons
- Stage 2 and 3 books

	Months	Language and Physical Characteristics of Baby	Types of Books to Read
Stage 5 *The Word* *Maker* Chapter 7	12–18	• Can *say* an average of forty words at sixteen months. *Understands* 100–150 words. • Uses a word in different contexts. For example, will say "duck" when he sees his rubber duckie in the bathtub, a picture of a duck in a book, or a real duck in a pond. • Uses a variety of intonation patterns when babbling or trying to speak. • Responds to your questions with pointing, body language, sounds, and some words in an attempt to have a conversation. • Memory is aided by the combination of rhymes or songs with movement, such as "Itsy Bitsy Spider." • Wants to do what he sees a parent doing: sweep the floor, give the dog a treat, or get a book and read it. • Crawls, climbs, and walks. Can crawl or walk to the bookcase and select favorite books.	• Books that reflect your toddler's experiences, such as making a peanut butter sandwich, playing with a balloon, or putting on rain or snow gear • Homemade books about routines and experiences using photos, drawings, or cutouts from catalogues or magazines • Books that use phrases such as *good-bye, thank you* • Books that ask questions • Books with simple narrative structure, strong characters, events, and resolutions • Books with rhymes and songs accompanied by hand movements • Books with one or two lines of rhythmic language on each page • Stage 2, 3, and 4 books

| Stage 6 *The Phrase Maker* Chapter 8 | 18–24 | • Understands about 200 words. Can *say* an average of 50–170 words.

• Imitates expressions such as "Oh, oh!"

• Begins to combine nouns and verbs to make two-word phrases or sentences.

• Begins to ask, "What's that?" Knows that objects have names. Can name family members.

• Surge of mental development at this age results in the ability to think, reason, and speak words more clearly. There is also an increase in physical ability: toddler runs faster, turns knobs, and turns pages in a book, one at a time.

• Learns the structure of language, such as how to form a question and the proper word order of sentences.

• Captivated by the intricate, detailed illustrations in books like those of Richard Scarry. | • Books about your toddler's current interests

• Books with interesting language that is just a little beyond the toddler's conversational language

• Books that include hand and body movements

• Books with numbers, colors, and vocabulary concepts

• Books with longer stories and more complicated rhymes and alliteration

• Books that show various feelings (happy, sad, angry, jealous)

• Stage 2, 3, 4, and 5 books |

CHAPTER 3

Stage 1: The Listener

*Introducing Books Before Birth and from
Birth to Two Months*

Amidst all the excitement and overwhelming emotions that surround the first hours after birth, you may find a few moments to introduce your baby to a short, soothing, rhyming book, like *Time for Bed* by Mem Fox. Why begin to read to your baby so soon? Your baby has heard his parents' voices for a good portion of your pregnancy. You may have even read to him before birth. If so, you might want to select the same book to read after birth as you read before birth. Your baby will be calmed and reassured as he listens to the sound of your voices, especially if you read the same book you read several times before birth.

Reading to a Newborn

The number one reason to read to baby soon after birth is to make your baby feel comfortable and loved in your undivided attention. The second reason is to begin a routine that will become a habit for both you and baby that will last for years to come. The third reason is to get dad involved in a key part of baby's brain and emotional development right from the start. Dad's participation in baby's daily reading routine not only will help baby develop good language, but will promote a close bond between father and baby.

In infancy, the first building block of literacy that is being developed is

Photo by Linda Posnick.

the ability to listen; thus we call this stage, between birth and two months, The Listener. The ability to listen will develop throughout your child's preschool years and will be the key to learning throughout life. Language is the principal medium through which most education is transmitted. Hearing is the most important sense because language development and learning depend on it.

When Is the Best Time to Read to a Newborn?

You can read just about any time. You can even read while baby is asleep because there is no difference between the brainwaves of a newborn who is asleep and one who is awake.[1] At birth, although it may appear that your baby is asleep, he can hear and be stimulated by sounds. So you may read and talk to your baby, even if he is asleep. Once you and your baby get accustomed to nursing, you will sometimes be able to read during nursing. As your baby matures, at around two or three months, you'll be reading during his alert, awake times.

When Will Parents Know Their Baby Is Responding to Read-Alouds?

After a few weeks you'll begin to notice that your baby responds with body movements when you talk and read to him. When parents talk directly

S
T
A
G
E
1

to their infant, he can move his legs and arms in synchrony with their speech. When you read to your baby, observe his arms and legs as you read. At this stage, reading Mother Goose rhymes or other poems with rhythm, alliteration, and rhyming words might elicit a bodily response in the form of a very alert look. Repeatedly reading the same or similar poetry for the first month of life will create brain connections (synapses) that positively affect your baby's language development.

Dad continues reading as infant falls asleep.

If parents keep a journal of baby's development, it's instructive to notice baby's reactions to being read to. The first month they may just be calmed. The second month you'll notice their alertness and their visual attraction to bold picture designs. By the third month, they are so accustomed to the reading routine, they expect to be read to, and wiggle their arms and legs in anticipation as you read with expression. Adding photos to your read-aloud journal, including the names of books you read, will make a wonderful gift for your child when he grows up or something for your child to share in kindergarten and first grade. This will be visual proof of your gift of literacy to your child. The real proof will be your child's reading and writing ability, extensive vocabulary, and love of learning.

Since baby's head needs to be supported, it's tricky to hold a book and a baby at the same time. Be sure you and baby are comfortable, whether you're in bed or in a chair or nursing rocker. Because of brain and head size, humans are born earlier and less developed than other mammals. This means that for a couple of months after birth, human infants need to be sheltered from overstimulation in the form of too many loud noises. It's best to talk to your baby without the disturbances of other background noise such as the television. Reading or talking to your baby in a dimly lit, quiet environment is best. Protect your baby from extensive, unhelpful noises. Noises that are too loud can actually damage your baby's hearing. Some everyday noises such as average traffic, a power lawn mower, or an alarm clock are too loud for your baby.

What Kinds of Things Should We Read to Our Newborn?

From birth to two months, parents can read aloud anything they like. The main point of reading to your baby at this stage is to allow baby to hear the mellifluous tones of your voice. You can read straight from the text, whether it is a magazine or Mother Goose rhymes. If your baby has fallen asleep, he will love the closeness and security of your voice, which he knows well since before birth. Even at birth, when you begin reading every day, baby will get used to it, and expect it as part of her daily routine. At the very beginning, there is no special way to read. All you have to do is read any way you like and notice your baby's reactions. Does your baby seem to prefer certain tones of voice? Or a book that you may have read aloud before birth? Begin at birth to observe your baby's responses when you read, and you will notice the subtle ways newborns absorb everything you say. As your baby grows, your observations will give you clues to the best books and ways to read aloud.

When this baby is born he will be familiar with dad's voice because baby will have been read to regularly before birth.

Reading to Your Baby Before Birth

We could have created another stage, called the Listener Before Birth, because the auditory system is fairly well developed by the sixth month of pregnancy. Your baby can hear your voice as well as music and other sounds in the womb. In fact, listening to outside stimuli while in the womb is necessary for good auditory development. Studies show that after birth babies recognize specific books, rhymes, or music heard in the womb before birth. These familiar sounds are emotionally comforting to babies. Reading to your baby before birth is good for both you and your baby, as it not only prepares his brain for language and learning, but helps you get into the read-aloud routine as well.

It's not too early to start your reading routine before the big day—but remember it's also never too late to start! Whether you are in your sixth month of pregnancy or your baby is six months old, use the stages (Chapters 3 to 8) to begin reading to your baby today.

How One Mother Calmed Her Baby Before and After Birth by Reading to Him

One mother told us that when she was about five months pregnant with her son who is now a teenager, she felt a great deal of discomfort when he began kicking. She noticed that when she read something aloud, the kicking would stop. So she read to her baby in utero every time he started kicking. After the birth of her baby, she noticed that when he became agitated or started to cry, he felt comforted by the sound of her voice. Needless to say, this mother continued reading until her son learned to read. He has always been at the top of his class and loves to read.

How a Father Calmed His Baby with His Voice Minutes After Birth

The day Brandon was born, as recalled by Grandma:

I was assigned to video Brandon's birth. His mother, who had an epidural, looked happy and regal and beautiful right up until the pushing began. Dad was close beside her, announcing contractions and encouraging her to push. Then, a little black head appeared, followed by a slippery red body all curled up. After what seemed an eternity, Brandon began to wail. The nurse whisked him away to a receiving station under a little heat lamp and began cleaning him up. I was so filled with emotion, I set the video camera down to wipe my eyes.

Dad kissed mom and asked if he could go meet his son who continued to let out gusty wails. She excused dad, and as he leaned in to see his newborn son, dad said, "Hi, Brandon, it's your dad." In mid wail, the baby stopped crying and gazed up into the face of his dad who went on to say, "Remember when I read to you in mommy's tummy? Do you remember we read *Green Eggs and Ham?*"

All the tension in Brandon's little body seemed to drain out as he hung on dad's every word. It was the most precious moment, and everyone in the room remembers it to this day. There was no question that the baby was reassured by hearing the voice of his dad, who had sent loving messages to him in the womb almost from the time he was conceived. The baby seemed to be saying, "Oh, there you are. It's you!"

We all continue to read to Brandon, who is now three. He has favorite books and snuggles up to be read to at least a couple of times a day. Going to the library to pick out new books is a favorite activity.

Characteristics: Birth to Two Months

Listening

- Startled by unexpected noises
- Will turn his head in the direction of a caregiver's voice
- Recognizes mother's voice and prefers it to the sounds of other adult voices
- Remembers and is calmed by rhymes, stories, and music heard before he was born
- Is able to identify the rhythm, tones, and sounds of his parents' language within the first week
- Can hear lower-tone voices and sounds better than higher tones
- Can't discriminate sounds like mom's reading voice if there is background noise like other loud voices or the television

Verbal

- Communicates needs by crying

Visual

- Has limited vision, and can only see objects eight to ten inches away
- Has poor color vision
- Prefers to look at a human face, especially mother's
- Sees black-and-white designs or photos
- Imitates the movements of his mother's mouth and tongue forty-five minutes after birth
- Has no binocular vision or depth perception
- Relies mostly on peripheral vision
- Can't detect small visual details

Motor

- Sleeps 75 percent of the time
- Has mostly reflexive movements, such as sucking or grasping

- Moves body in synchrony with adult speech; coordinates his arms and legs and moves them at the speed and rhythm of what he hears
- Can form a grin (beginning smile) in response to faces at three weeks
- Turns toward or away from a person or event

Step-by-Step Read-Aloud Instructions: Birth to Two Months

Select a book from the recommended list at the end of this chapter.

How to hold baby—getting ready

- Choose a time and place that is quiet and free of distracting noises.
- Select whatever you want to read: rhyming books, your favorite parenting magazines, or the newspaper.
- Make yourself comfortable with your baby in your rocker or glider with a boppy (nursing pillow), in bed propped up with pillows, or on the couch.
- Read for a few minutes at least twice a day when your baby is alert and has been fed. You can also read while you are nursing. You may also continue reading if your baby falls asleep.
- If you have other children, read what they like while you are holding your baby.
- When your newborn opens his eyes, hold him close to you (eight to ten inches) so he can look at your face as you read.

Parentese interaction

- Try to vary the pace, phrasing, voice rhythms, and pitch, emphasizing certain words (see discussion of "parentese" in Chapter 2).
- Observe how your baby's movements synchronize with your voice when you read.

Challenges

- Finding the right time to read when baby is comfortable. Fussiness is sometimes caused by baby's immature digestive system. Changing position, burping, or waiting a few minutes can alleviate discomfort, and then you can resume reading.
- Finding time to read when you do not have to do other things. Try reading to the baby while nursing.

- Holding baby in a way that supports his head and book at same time. Try using pillows, or laying the baby next to you on a bed.
- Feeling silly reading to what appears to be an unresponsive baby. It helps to interject talking to your baby while reading, as if you are having a personal conversation (see Read-Aloud Demonstration below of father reading to his six-week-old baby).
- Your baby falls asleep. You may continue to read.
- Your baby gets easily distracted. Make sure that background noise is limited by turning off the television, lowering volume of music, and keeping other voices at a minimum.

Read-Aloud Demonstration: Father Reading to His Six-Week-Old Baby

This six-week-old baby already has a read-aloud routine. After being nursed, dad changes her diaper, and takes her to their favorite read-aloud chair. Dad enjoys reading his daughter nursery rhymes, and he makes sure that she knows that what he is reading is especially for her. Before, during, and after reading the rhymes, Dad tells his baby what rhyme he is reading and says, "This is for you, Little P." (Dad called baby "Little P" while she was in utero; it stood for "Little Person," since he did not know sex or name of baby, and he contin-

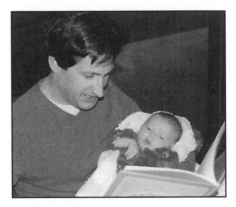

ued to call her that for a while after she was born.) He is aware of her colicky stomach discomfort but he continues reading because she is used to it and is actually soothed and comforted by it.

(The italicized words indicate the rhymes dad reads. The rest is a "conversation" using parentese. He adds his own words to the text in order to lovingly interact with his baby.)

Dad: Are you ready? This one is for Kaia (the name of his baby girl).

"The Cat and the Fiddle"
Hey diddle, diddle,

The cat and the fiddle,
The cow jumped over the moon;
The little dog laughed

(Dad laughs in response to baby's grunting noises. Then he finishes the rhyme and continues reading.)

Hey, "Little P." Let's try this one again, when you are not pooping.

(Dad reads the same rhyme again. He reads slowly, pausing and enunciating clearly.)

Let's try "Baa, Baa, Black Sheep."

Baa, baa, black sheep,
Have you any wool?

(Dad continues reading the rhyme as baby looks back and forth from the book to his face.)

Let's read this one.

"Diddle, Diddle, Dumpling"
Diddle, diddle, dumpling, my son John

(Dad finishes that rhyme and continues reading "Humpty Dumpty Sat on a Wall" and "Peter Peter, Pumpkin Eater.")

Let's read "Lucy Locket," Sweet P.

(Baby gurgles and starts grunting again. Dad continues reading "Lucy Locket.")

Listen, Sweet P.

"Jack Be Nimble"
Jack be Nimble
Jack be quick

(Baby is uncomfortable. She squirms and grunts as she appears to be having a bowel movement. Grandma interjects, "Do you think she's tired? Has she had enough?" To which dad responds, "No, she is just pooping, so she's uncomfortable." He keeps reading.)

Jack jumped over
The candle stick.

(Dad reads "Little Bo-Peep" and "Sing a Song of Sixpence.")

Want to hear this one, Little P?

There Was a Little Girl.

(Dad reads the rhyme as baby calmly listens.)

What do you think about that, Little P?

(Dad continues reading one more rhyme after baby falls asleep.)[2]

What to Notice in the Read-Aloud Demonstrations

Notice how the father:

- Holds baby during their reading time. At this young age babies are very flexible and are comfortable in a variety of positions. At this stage babies don't need to see the book. However, if positioned near parent's face, some babies will look intently at parent's face as they listen to parent read.

- Reads from the text and then adds a few comments on the side. "OK this one is for Kaia. OK let's try this one again, Little P."

- Follows his baby's lead. He keeps reading, although his baby seems fussy. Grandma asks if they should stop since the baby seems uncomfortable, to which dad responds, "No, she's fine; she's just pooping." Dad's voice is actually soothing to her during her typical baby digestive discomforts.

- Reads rhymes because their rhyme and rhythm are soothing to baby's ears.

- Cuddles and creates a closeness, which will become part of their daily reading routine.

- Continues to read even though baby falls asleep. Dad's voice soothed baby to sleep. She can still hear his soothing voice.

Characteristics of Stage 1 Books

Even if you read to your baby before birth, it's a thrill to read aloud for the first time after birth. It's an occasion that merits a photograph for baby's album so that when your baby is grown, he'll see that you wasted no time in giving him the gift of language and the love of reading.

Although newborns' limited range of vision allows them to look at bright, bold patterns, the most effective books for this stage feature rhymes or pages

S
T
A
G
E
1

filled with chantable rhythms so your baby can hear your voice. Having heard you in utero, your baby feels comfortable and secure when you speak. Any children's book you particularly like will probably be welcomed by your newborn. Some books with nursery rhymes or titles like *Chicka Chicka Boom Boom* may become favorites for the next few years.

Recommended Types of Books: Birth to Two Months

- Books with rhymes
- Books read aloud before baby was born
- Your favorite children's books
- Board books with black-and-white patterns
- Any reading matter of interest to you

Baby Book Reviews at-a-Glance: With Parentese Tips and Illustration Talking Points

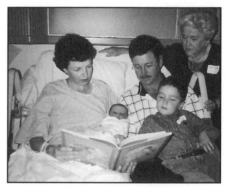

Tomie's Little Mother Goose
Tomie dePaola
Board book
G.P. Putnam's Sons, 32 pages, 1997

Mother Goose books come in a variety of formats and have been illustrated by various artists. One of our favorites is Tomie dePaola's version. Your newborn will love

Hours after birth in the hospital room, newborn listens to his first read-aloud, a routine already established with his older brother.

the sound of your voice as you read, sing, or chant many favorite Mother Goose rhymes. Tomie dePaola is a prolific author-illustrator, a favorite among preschool and primary school teachers. You might look for other editions of dePaola's Mother Goose rhymes in a lightweight paperback book.

PARENTESE TIPS AND TALKING POINTS ABOUT THE ILLUSTRATIONS:

- You could start with the familiar "This little pig went to market." While touching each of baby's toes, you can change the tone and volume of your voice with each line, and then squeak out "and this little pig cried wee-wee," and so on.

- What responses can you observe in a newborn? Depending on your infant baby's waking or sleeping state, you may see that your baby appears alert, or that he moves in synchrony with your speech. Responses may be very subtle at first. But know that every word you speak to your precious newborn is being registered in baby's active, growing brain. The more you are tuned in to your baby, the more you'll notice.

How A Baby Grows
Nola Buck, illustrated by Pamela Paparone
Board book
Harper Festival,® 14 pages, 1998

This book achieves two things: It gives your baby a nice rhyme to hear while you are helping teach your older child what to expect from his newborn sibling. The book tells what baby does, sees, needs, the way he speaks, the things he hears, what he shares and knows, and how he grows. The illustrations are clear and colorful, and good for baby or toddler. Your toddler at one or one-and-a-half may also like this book, as many toddlers enjoy books about babies.

PARENTESE TIPS AND TALKING POINTS ABOUT THE ILLUSTRATIONS:

- If you bring baby's older sibling to the hospital for a peek at new baby, gather your family around you while holding your newborn and read page one. Use the text as a starting point to explain to an older sibling what babies do, like crying and the need for diaper changing and so on. Older children may not understand that babies communicate by crying. You can have a conversation with baby's sibling(s) about crying, and when to expect it.

- During all this conversation, you can look at your infant, and say something like, "We're telling your brother (or sister) all about you. We are so happy you are here. We'll have so much fun reading together." Your older child, even if he can't read, might want to make up the words to the pictures, and "read" to your infant.

The Baby's Lap Book
Kay Chorao
Hardcover
Dutton Children's Books, 58 pages, 1990

Book cover: *The Baby's Lap Book*

We love this book because of the sweet, happy illustrations and the many traditional nursery rhymes that many parents heard from their parents. These nursery rhymes are part of the European tradition handed down for generations. Every culture has its own version in its own language. Maintain your family's traditions by singing, chanting, or saying your own nursery rhymes in your native language. As your child grows, nursery rhymes form a staple of lyrical language, content, and beloved memories found nowhere else. (This is the book used in the demonstration of father reading to his baby earlier in this chapter.)

PARENTESE TIPS AND TALKING POINTS ABOUT THE ILLUSTRATIONS:

- Start with rhymes you know and are comfortable with, like "Pat-A-Cake." Though your baby is still too young to participate, you can clap your hands and move rhythmically, observing your baby watch your every move. Soon he will be like the toddler in the illustration, clapping with you.

- Sing the familiar "Baa, Baa, Black Sheep," or chant "It's Raining, it's Pouring." Your newborn will love the sound of your voice. He will look at your mouth and face with total absorption.

Time for Bed
Mem Fox, illustrated by Jane Dyer
Board book, lap-sized board book
Harcourt, 27 pages, 1997

Book cover: *Time for Bed*

You can start reading this lyrical book even before birth and continue through the toddler years. The gentle rhymes about mother animals and their babies are sure to have a soporific effect on your baby. We recommend that you pack this compact little board book with your things to take to the hospital to read the day your baby is born. Mem Fox is one of the world's greatest authors of children's books for all ages. As your baby grows, he will enjoy her many other titles.

PARENTESE TIPS AND TALKING POINTS ABOUT THE ILLUSTRATIONS:

- For a newborn, there are several ways you can read this book. You can read it straight through in a regular voice while your baby is either awake or asleep.

- You can also start at the first page with the intention of trying out your "parentese" through the voices of the animals.
  After reading, "It's time for bed, little mouse, little mouse, darkness is falling all over the house," you can interject something like, "Can you hear the little baby mouse go squeak, squeak, squeak?" in a squeaky voice. Here you are already starting questioning, and you're using an expressive voice to get and maintain baby's attention. You can ask similar questions and make animal noises all the way through the book. In this way, you are already dialoguing with baby and giving him the opportunity to hear many, many more words than just those provided by the book.

Fingerplays and Songs for the Very Young
Illustrated by Carolyn Croll
Board book
Random House, 22 pages, 2001

This book will be your "ace in the hole" throughout your baby's first two years. It gives you beautifully illustrated, well-known rhymes, songs, and directions for finger and hand motions. Your baby craves such active attention. Such classics as "Pat-a-Cake," "Open, Shut Them," "This Little Piggy," "Ring Around the Rosie," and "Wheels on the Bus" will keep your baby enchanted. No baby should be without the experience of classic finger play rhymes. They are part of the formation of your child's literacy. If you can't find this book, look for other books that give you instructions under each rhyme on what to do with baby's hands, feet, or body. Books with finger plays for infants are different than those for preschoolers. The instructions for older toddlers teach them how to do the hand motions. For infants, parents will need to manipulate their baby's fingers or toes, etc. For example, for a familiar rhyme like "This Little Piggy," parents would gently grasp each of baby's toes and wiggle them while chanting the rhyme.

PARENTESE TIPS AND TALKING POINTS ABOUT THE ILLUSTRATIONS:

- For newborns, we especially recommend "Shoe the Little Horse," "This Little Piggy," and "Cobbler, Cobbler." Each of these rhymes has instructions that involve patting or holding baby's feet or toes while looking into baby's eyes. In infancy, playing with baby's feet is easy and gentle.

- Every rhyme tells you exactly what to do while chanting the rhyme. You can place the book on the bed next to your baby so you can read the rhyme and directions while holding baby's feet.

Hippety-Hop Hippety-Hay: Growing with Rhymes from Birth to Age Three
Opal Dunn, illustrated by Sally Anne Lambert
Hardcover
Henry Holt and Company, 46 pages, 1999

This book is divided into developmental stages that are similar to those in *Baby Read-Aloud Basics.* The poems were written for the youngest babies through age three, making the selection process easy for parents. Parents tell us that the brevity of the rhymes holds baby's attention. Most of the poems and songs include actions using your hands or fingers, a feature babies love. The attractive illustrations show parents going through the motions described in the poems. Some of the rhymes are set to folk melodies whose musical notations are included in the back of the book.

We recommend this book as a perfect choice for a shower gift, because it shows parents how to read the poems and discusses the importance of starting a reading routine from birth. Also look for Opal Dunn's new book, *Number Rhymes to Say and Play*, available in paperback.

PARENTESE TIPS AND TALKING POINTS ABOUT THE ILLUSTRATIONS:

- For infancy, the first pages include rhymes that encourage you to touch your baby as you talk:

STAGE 1

These are baby's fingers
These are baby's toes
This is baby's belly button
Round and round it goes.

- Other poems encourage you to sing or chant. How your baby will love listening to your voice reciting these verses over and over again! Repetition is good for your baby's brain, and it's also comforting.

Chicka Chicka Boom Boom
Bill Martin, Jr., illustrated by Lois Ehlert
Hardcover
Simon and Schuster, 30 pages, 1989

Why do we recommend an alphabet book for a newborn? Because we don't think of this fast-paced rollicking rhyme as an alphabet book until preschool age. For an infant, the letters are just a blur. But the unique rhythm of the sounds will be a cause for joy. Your child will enjoy the rhymes and Lois Ehlert's bold, primary-colored graphics through first grade. Parents will hear themselves chanting some of the verse in their heads as they go about their daily business: "Chicka chicka boom boom! Will there be enough room?"

PARENTESE TIPS AND TALKING POINTS ABOUT THE ILLUSTRATIONS:

- You may read this repetitively. Your baby loves to hear the same words again and again. By the time your baby reaches the age of two, he will know much of the rhyme by heart and may even be interested in some of the letters.

- Since the rhyme demands to be read at a lively pace, you'll find yourself having to turn pages quickly. We recommend reading the book while your baby is lying comfortably and safely on a blanket on the floor or bed. As your baby matures, be sure your baby can see the illustrations. Another way is to position your baby upright in a portable baby car seat or bouncer. You can hold the book so it's visible to you and to baby, and you can easily flip pages.

- This is one of the few books that we recommend for which you don't interject your own words, as the pace of the rhyme demands that you move right along from beginning to end. It's impossible to interrupt the driving rhythm of the cadence. However, you can be as expressive as you please. It's sure to hold your baby's attention.

Baby Dance
Ann Taylor, illustrated by Marjorie van Heerden
Board book
Harper Festival, 14 pages, 1999

This will be one of your baby's ongoing favorites through all the stages from birth to two. Parents will have as much fun as baby because it's impossible to read without chanting, accompanied by rhythmic movements. "Dance, little baby, move to and fro." The fabulous, colorful illustrations of dad and baby by Marjorie van Heerden make you want to move just by looking at them. As your baby matures he will smile, coo, and wiggle when you chant and go through the motions. As soon as he's able to talk, he'll say, "Read it again."

PARENTESE TIPS AND TALKING POINTS ABOUT THE ILLUSTRATIONS:

- If you begin reading this book at birth, gently sway your baby to and fro while reading, then as baby matures you can move around a little more and dance and sing. Soon your baby will be laughing out loud like the baby in the book.

- Some of the actions you see in the book are the types that dads love to do with their baby's. This book is an excellent example of how dad can be involved with baby, giving mom a break so she can rest. See Chapter 10 for more activities dads can do with their babies. Babies get a special thrill when they read and play with them.

Sleepytime Rhyme
Remy Charlip
Hardcover
Greenwillow Books, 23 pages, 1999

This book is a living celebration between parent and baby. *Sleepytime Rhyme* will be a favorite throughout the first two years. As your baby grows, he will cuddle and relax when you read in a soft tone of voice. Babies love to look at the mommies and babies in each of the joyful, vividly colored illustrations. This would be a welcome baby shower book.

PARENTESE TIPS AND TALKING POINTS ABOUT THE ILLUSTRATIONS:

- From the moment of birth parents can read (or sing to the tune *Twinkle, Twinkle, Little Star*). "I love your hair, your head, your chin . . ." while touching and gazing at your newborn miracle.

- Read it through yourself first, and then put the book down and look at your baby and tell him everything you love about him. You might say everything differently each time you read. If baby grunts, or makes any response, you can acknowledge these responses as part of the conversation. For example, "I love your coos, I love your grunts, I love you here, I love you there," etc.

¡Pio Peep!
Selected by Alma Flor Ada and Isabel Campoy
Hardcover, Paperback, and CD
HarperCollins, 64 pages, 2003

These traditional Spanish nursery rhymes are among the most popular in Spanish-speaking countries. Spanish-speaking parents and grandparents will remember these rhymes from their childhood. Alma Flor Ada, a well-known author of children's books in both English and Spanish, selected them. Most of the Spanish rhymes have established and well-known chant-like rhythms. Babies will soon grow to recognize and love these familiar sounds. Each Spanish rhyme includes an English translation that works well for parents using parentese in English. If you read the well-translated and recreated rhymes in English, you can make up your own rhythms.

PARENTESE TIPS AND TALKING POINTS ABOUT THE ILLUSTRATIONS:

- You may read the rhymes repetitively because repetition helps baby to learn the rhythm and sounds of her home language. If the home language is mainly Spanish, baby will learn to recognize her parent's native language. The more words she hears in Spanish, the easier it will be for her to learn English. Chapter 9 discusses why a strong foundation in the first home language supports learning a second language.

- Don't let the fact that the book offers Hispanic folkloric rhymes in Spanish dissuade you from reading the English translations. This book is not just for children of Hispanic heritage, but can expand your baby's repertoire of delightful sounds and subjects. As your baby grows, his maturing vision will love the strong and colorful illustrations. Rhymes such as "The Piñata," "The Little Ant," "In My Backyard," and "The White Horse" are sure to gain a whole new international group of baby and toddler fans.

CHAPTER 4

Stage 2: The Observer

Reading to Your Visual Two- to Four-Month-Old

Reading to a two- to four-month-old is a treat. It's never too late (or too early!) to start nourishing your baby's brain with the words she needs to build a solid language foundation.

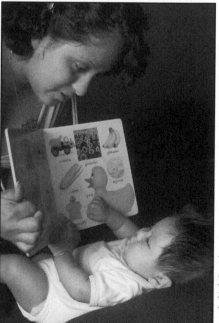

Every word you read and speak to your baby is a gift of language—a gift that all babies require for a full and happy life. In addition, when you read to your baby at this age, you'll feel a special bonding through books that delights both you and your baby. The intimacy of reading aloud is something your baby will expect every day right along with nursing, sleeping, and bathing.

During the second and third month, your baby's world begins to expand. Feeling comfortable and secure in her surroundings, she begins to smile and become more social as her visual field lengthens. We call your child at

Photo by Linda Posnick.

this stage the Observer, because she is now observing as intently as she listens. You'll notice that your baby can lock her gaze into yours for many minutes at a time. This connection between parent and baby is crucial for baby's development and pure delight for mom, dad, and grandparents. At this stage babies can perceive bold colors and can see details more clearly. Their binocular vision and depth perception is quickly improving. The illustrations that baby can now perceive in board books will stimulate and help improve visual skills. When you read to your baby at this young age, you are promoting both language and visual skill development.[1]

If your baby is positioned so she can see your face and the book, here are some of the things you'll see your baby doing. Your baby is now so alert that she'll be looking back and forth between the book and your expressive face as you talk and read. Although she won't understand the meanings of the words you're saying, she will connect with your mood and emotional tone. You will have fun noticing your baby's reaction to the way you dramatize a story. She may show her excitement and glee by breathing faster, vigorously shaking her arms, and looking back and forth between your face and the bold designs of the book. Your baby's verbal responses to your reading and talking will be in the form of sweet little coos and grunts. She'll also attempt to imitate your talking by moving her mouth in as many ways as possible.

Reading-aloud during Stage 2 focuses on "dialoguing," or taking turns "talking" to each other. Every parent of babies around this age knows the joys of the back and forth verbal as well as nonverbal interaction. This back and forth interaction that sometimes includes questioning is the basis for future social conversational skills.

The intimate dialoguing between you and baby not only promotes attachment but is part of the way your baby learns how to identify her home language in the first months. Babies can actually distinguish between the language of their parents and other languages. Babies listen to volume, pitch, and rhythm at this stage, and it's these qualities that help them identify the language spoken at home.

You'll be amazed at the length of your two- to four-month-old's attention span during read-aloud time, if she is alert and has been fed and changed. In this stage it is best if you speak in whole sentences so baby can absorb the flavor, rhythm, and tone of your language. At a later stage when your baby is keyed into meanings, you'll emphasize words more.

You may notice that no matter what kind of mood you are in, the ritual of reading to your baby has a mood-elevating effect on you. Your baby's happy responses to the lighthearted, joyful messages of baby books are communicated by your enthusiastic parentese reading style. Your baby's smiles and coos cancel out all other concerns you may have had before you started reading. After your reading session, both parent and baby are happy and satisfied.

The books recommended at the end of this chapter are all appropriate for the characteristics of the two- to four-month stage of development. You'll find books with bright, simple illustrations designed for your baby's developing visual capabilities. The rhythmic rhymes and chants will give your baby practice listening to the flavor of her own language, while providing an opportunity for parent and baby "conversation." Begin today to experience the joys of reading to your baby!

Characteristics: Two to Four Months

Listening

- Responds more positively to parentese than regular speech tone (see Chapter 2). You can gain her attention by changing the pitch, rhythm, and volume of your voice.
- Loves to be talked to about whatever you are doing, such as changing her diaper or cooking a meal.
- Likes to listen to lullabies, classical, and other calming music appropriate for babies.
- Can't discriminate sounds, like mom's reading voice, if there is background noise like other loud voices or the television.

Verbal

- Begins to "take turns" in conversations by cooing when mother stops talking.
- Develops expressive laughter.
- Cries less, and there are more coo's and gurgles.

Visual

- Extends range of visual focus to eighteen inches.
- Can now follow movement of mobiles.
- Sees checkerboard patterns and bright, contrasting colors.
- Begins developing binocular vision and depth perception.
- Can see more details in book illustrations and in the environment.

- Likes bold, black-and-white designs or illustrations featuring bright colors.
- Becomes more socially interactive. Makes extended eye contact and gives genuine smiles as she becomes more alert.

Motor

- Tries to reach out to objects that she sees; however, lacks the coordination to grasp them.
- Able to move head from one side to the other while tracking a person's movement.
- Can lift chin and chest up if placed on her stomach.
- Can play with own hands and suck fingers and fists.

Step-by-Step Read-Aloud Instructions: Two to Four Months

Select a book from the recommended list at the end of this chapter.

How to position baby: Getting ready

- A favorite position is to place baby on her back on a flat surface (bed or floor). You lie next to baby supported by your arm, holding the book with the other hand so that baby can see the book and your face.

Mom reads to baby snuggled in a sling.

- Using a boppy around your waste (pillow commonly used for breast feeding), place baby on boppy next to your chest as if nursing. This frees hands to comfortably hold book and turn pages.
- Hold baby upright facing outward against your chest, wrapping arms around baby and holding book with your hands. In this position baby can see only the book.
- Experiment with ways of holding baby so she can look at both your face as well as the book.

Baby is positioned so he can see both the book and dad's face.

- Place your baby in a sling. When seated, baby is resting on your !ap and can look between your face and the book. Your hands are free to hold book.

Parentese interaction

- As you read, change the pitch, volume, and speed of your reading as you react to her facial expressions (see discussion of "parentese" in Chapter 2).
- Look into your baby's eyes. Say her name and lovingly talk in response to her baby sounds.
- Try a variety of sing-song voice rhythms emphasizing certain words. You might also try singing.
- In order to capitalize on your baby's increasing social interactivity, pause as you read, respond to your baby's coo's, and make eye contact.

Challenges

- If your baby wants to grasp what you are reading, allow her to do so. You could occasionally introduce cloth books (although these books usually do not have as high-quality language as paper books).

- If your baby becomes fussy, try changing positions, burping, or get up and walk baby around, talking as you walk, then resume reading.
- If you have older children, read what they like while you hold your baby.
- At this stage baby is heavier and still can't support her head, so finding a comfortable position is even more challenging than Stage 1. One of the best positions is to place baby on her back on the bed or the floor so baby can see both the book and your face.
- If baby falls asleep you may continue to read.

S
T
A
G
E

2

Read-Aloud Demonstration: Mother Reading to Her Three-Month-Old Baby

After nursing, Fernando enjoys being on his back while mother leans over him, face to face, holding the book so it is easy to see. In this position, he can look at the book and also look at mom's face as she reads and talks.

Mom is using parentese by reading with a lot of expression, changing the pitch of her voice and speeding up and slowing down as she reads. There are pauses in her reading to give the baby time to respond. If he is excited about a page, his breathing accelerates or his hand tries to reach out to touch something on the page. In addition, he looks intently for longer periods of time or vocalizes when something

attracts his attention. Finally, when he is tired or not interested in a page, he turns away. Mom adapts her reading to his reactions. Although he is not saying words, his attempts at vocal coo's, goo's, and uhs amount to a two-way conversation. Fernando and his mother are engaging in early conversation!

The following is an excerpt of mother reading to her three-month-old. Notice how many more words mom speaks to baby than the actual sixty-six words of the text of the book. This illustrates how books serve as a platform to launch dialogue between mother and baby—hundreds and hundreds of words that nourish baby's language development.

(Words that are read the way they appear in the book are italicized. All the other words not in italics are mom's own words.)

Mom: Look, *Bunny's First Snow Flake.* Where is the bunny? Let's see what's here. Haa! Look at the bunny. *Cold wind blows. Swoosh, whoosh. Winter is coming soon.*

> (Baby is reaching out to touch the white bunny on the page.)

That's the bunny, the white bunny. Where's the pumpkin? There's a big pumpkin, and that's a raccoon.

> (Mom uses less exaggerated parentese when reading the text directly
> out of the book. Mom asks questions based on what Fernando is
> touching.)

Yes, do you want to grab the bunny? Touch his nose. Touch his nose.

> (Mom holds Fernando's hand and helps him touch the bunny's nose.)

Look at the bunny. Let's see what else is here.

　(Mom turns the page.)

Look—a snowflake! Is everyone ready for winter? What are you going to touch now? The mouse. Where is the little mouse? Look at the little mouse right there, and that's a raccoon.

> (Mom speaks in a high-pitched voice and points, holding Fernando's
> hand.)

What else do you see? (Mom pauses) Do you like those colors? Look at those colors. That's orange. See the bunny jumping?

> (Fernando is pulling at the book as if wanting to turn the page.)

Do you want to turn the page?

> (Mom turns the page.)

Bunny is hiding behind a tree. Look at his loooooong ears.

> (She guides his hand up along the long ears. Baby makes a grunting
> sound.)

Yes, you want to talk now? Do you want to read with me?

　. . . and so on. Mom reads and talks through the entire book like this.

　When we were finished with this particular book, we continued videotaping Fernando's reading of several other books. It wasn't until later that evening, when we reviewed the videotape, that we realized Fernando had been listening for over twenty-five minutes and was engaged the entire time. His attention span at fourteen weeks exceeded that of our kindergartners and first graders who have never been read to.[2]

What to Notice in the Read-Aloud Demonstration

Notice how the mother:

- Sits facing her baby so that baby can look back and forth between her face and the illustrations.
- Does not read text as it appears; mom interjects her own words related to book text.
- Adjusts the text to the toddler. She also speaks in parentese by using an excited, animated voice that sometimes pauses, slows down, or increases in volume to capture Fernando's attention.
- Uses less exaggerated parentese when reading the words directly out of the book, and how she looks back and forth between the baby and the book.
- Engages in conversation by taking turns listening to baby sounds and then responding to baby.
- Asks questions and allows waiting time so that baby can respond with an excited breath, a coo, or a grunt.
- Follows the baby's lead by asking questions based on the picture the baby is touching.
- Helps baby to physically interact with the book by holding his hand and helping him touch the illustrations or make scratch noises (even though his hands are still clasped and unable to point.)
- Responds positively when baby tries to grasp book. Mother asks him if he would like to turn the page (which he physically can't do yet, since his fists are clasped, and he does not have the coordination). Then mom turns the page.
- Reads a book appropriate for this stage. The book mother selects has rhyming language and bold, colorful illustrations.
- Uses the book's topics to teach concepts such as colors, animal names, description of specific animal features, and objects.

See "Baby Book Reviews at a Glance" below for more ideas on what to talk about when reading this book and others.

Characteristics of Stage 2 Books

Not only is your precious baby becoming cuter by the minute, she's also developing a wider visual and social awareness. Books that have bold, contrasting, black-and-white illustrations or bright and colorful designs are the best choices for babies at this stage. In addition, your baby enjoys the rhythm and emotion heard in your voice from books with rhymes or those that can be dramatized with laughter or hand motions like *Clap Hands* or *Counting Kisses*. Your baby is learning the first steps in the give and take of "conversation" that the following books help promote.

Many of these books lend themselves to hand motions and physically touching and playing with your baby. The challenge is to find a position that allows baby to be placed in a car seat, sling, or on a bed to free your hands for the hand motions. Your baby should be close enough to see clearly both your face, hand movements, and the book illustrations.

If you're just beginning to read to your baby for the first time at two to four months, we suggest that you add some or all of the books from Stage 1, since they include many well-known nursery rhymes that will become your baby's favorites for years to come. They can now enjoy looking at the illustrations in some of these rhyming books. At every stage you'll be adding some of the books suggested in the "Baby Book Reviews at a Glance" section. By two years of age, your child will have a library of books that can be enjoyed and shared through the preschool years and beyond!

Recommended Types of Books: Two to Four Months

- Wordless picture books
- Rhyming and song books
- Board books with contrasting primary colors or bold black-and-white designs
- Books you read to baby before birth
- Soft cloth books
- Books that can be chanted with rhythm

Baby Book Reviews at a Glance

White on Black
Tana Hoban
Board book
Greenwillow Books, 10 pages, 1993
Available in Spanish and French

This is a wordless picture book featuring wonderful, large, white silhouettes on a black background. Two- to four-month-olds (as well as newborns whose vision is just developing) can easily see the bold images: a bottle, a rocking horse, a sailboat, a rubber duck, buttons, a string of beads, a bird, a flower, an apple, and a banana. You'll be amazed at how focused and alert your baby will be in response to these images.

PARENTESE TIPS AND TALKING POINTS ABOUT THE ILLUSTRATIONS:

- Not only can mom or dad (sister, brother, grandparent, or caretaker) name each object, but they can also have fun making a "dialogue" based on the pictures. "Look at the buttons! See Mommy's buttons?" or "Look at the bird! Where will he fly?" etc. Your baby in one short "reading" session will be hearing hundreds and hundreds of words. Think of it as food for the brain.

- Although any of the recommended books can be talked about using any language, this totally baby-oriented, wordless picture book obviously speaks to babies of all languages. So whether you speak French, Spanish, Chinese, or Korean, your words, language, and culture will speak through this effective little black-and-white book.

Polar Bear, Polar Bear, What Do You Hear?
Bill Martin Jr., illustrated by Eric Carle
Board book
Henry Holt and Company, 24 pages, 1991
Available in Spanish and French

A famous author and illustrator team up to produce a rhyming chant that will be read time and again through kindergarten. Based on the universally popular *Brown Bear, Brown Bear, What Do You See?* by Bill Martin Jr., *Polar*

Bear is about the sounds animals make when they communicate. All those wonderful words for animal sounds are listed at the end of the book: growling, roaring, snorting, etc. Eric Carle's colorful, painted tissue paper, cutout pictures are bold enough to capture the gaze of any two- to four-month-old.

PARENTESE TIPS AND TALKING POINTS ABOUT THE ILLUSTRATIONS:

- Read the rhyme for one of the animals, and as you turn the page, make the sound of that animal as you look tenderly into your baby's eyes. Your baby will smile as she listens to the rhythm and tone of your voice as you dramatize each of the animal sounds.

- You can start pointing out features of the animals: "Wow, look at the long claws on the bear."

My Aunt Came Back
Pat Cummings
Board book
Harper Festival, 14 pages, 1998

We recommend this joyful book for two- to four-month-olds because of the singsongy rhythm of the language.

A fun dramatization can accompany the chant-like rhyme of each page, so that after repeated readings, your baby will begin to expect the action that accompanies each rhyming page. In addition to the spirited rhymes, the simple illustrations are bright, colorful, and happy. Your baby will grow with *My Aunt Came Back* to eighteen months and beyond.

PARENTESE TIPS AND TALKING POINTS ABOUT THE ILLUSTRATIONS:

- When you read the rhyme, you can hold, wiggle, and kiss your baby's little foot (shoes).

- On every page the last word of every stanza has something aunt brings back that you can dramatize, like the ring. Touch your baby's ring finger.

- When you read, say the word "back" a little louder. The word "back" appears at the end of the first and third line of every stanza throughout the book. When you say "back," look away from the book and into your baby's eyes and smile. Watch her reaction. After a few readings, she'll expect your smiley face when you read "back."

S
T
A
G
E

2

Playtime, Maisy
Lucy Cousins
Cloth
Candlewick Press, 6 pages, 2001
Available in Spanish and French

Maisy is an adorable mouse who is featured in many board books and paperback titles by Lucy Cousins, such as *Maisy's Favorite Animals, Maisy Goes to School, Maisy's Bedtime, Maisy's ABC, Happy Birthday Maisy*, and many more. Open this cloth book to any page, and you'll see why your baby's eyes will be riveted on the simple, colorful illustrations. This particular Maisy book is wordless. That means parents can talk about the mouse, Maisy, and what she is doing. Cousins' artwork exudes a sense of joy, a quality we all want children exposed to. We selected a quality cloth book for this stage because it's light, soft, and can be put in baby's mouth. It's also washable, an important feature when baby puts it in her mouth. Toward the end of this stage your baby will be trying to handle the book and also teething.

Book cover: *Playtime, Maisy*

PARENTESE TIPS AND TALKING POINTS ABOUT THE ILLUSTRATIONS:

- Use this wordless book to talk about what Maisy is doing in the illustrations: "Look, Maisy's putting sand from her pail into the dump truck. Look, Maisy is zooming down the slide, weeee!"

- Talk about Maisy's long, skinny tail as you slide your finger around the tail. Finding the tail on each page could be an activity in itself. Or you can point to her black noise, protruding snout, or whiskers.

- Regardless of what you talk about, make it interesting by using catching exclamatory terms like, "Look!" or "Wow." Use a variety of tones and volumes. Be playful and have fun. Your voice and the bright illustrations will hold your baby's attention.

STAGE 2

What's on My Head?
Margaret Miller
Board book
Simon and Schuster, 12 pages, 1998

This is part of a series entitled *Look Baby Books*, appropriate for baby's first year. Your baby will love the huge, close-up photographs of bright-eyed babies with cute, fuzzy animals or a rubber duck or hats on their heads. There are only eleven words, but many more words will be exchanged between you and your baby as a result of the interest and smiles generated by these captivating photos. Other titles by Margaret Miller are *Peekaboo Baby, Baby Faces, Baby Food,* and *Get Ready Baby, Boo! Baby.*

PARENTESE TIPS AND TALKING POINTS ABOUT THE ILLUSTRATIONS:

- These photos open the door for creating a game out of putting fun objects like a rubber ducky or different kinds of hats on your head. As baby grows she will laugh when you put things on her head also. This is another way of creating occasions for dialogue and interplay using a variety of vocabulary words inspired by this fun book.

- Ask questions: "Where's the baby's nose?" and "Where's your nose?" Ask questions about all the facial features in the photographs as you touch your baby's face.

Bunny's First Snowflake
Monica Wellington
Board book
Dutton Children's Books,
22 pages, 2000

The expressive, sonorous language, like "Bustle, rustle. Scratch, scratch," will capture your baby's attention. This is one of the unique books in which both the flowing story words and the illustrations will captivate a two- to four-month-old baby. But you

Book cover: *Bunny's First Snowflake*

won't just read the words and turn the page, because there are so many interesting colorful creatures and objects to look at and talk about. Your baby will hear many more words than the sixty-six words of written text in the story. This book lends itself to asking lots of questions, a kind of verbal interaction that is good for your baby's language development. Monica Wellington also wrote *All My Little Ducklings* and *Bunny's Rainbow Day*. (This is the book used in the demonstration of the mother reading to her baby earlier in this chapter.)

PARENTESE TIPS AND TALKING POINTS ABOUT THE ILLUSTRATIONS:

- Every time you turn the page, ask, "Where's the mouse"? Then you wait a minute and say, "Look, the mouse is in the tree." As your baby grows, she will later be able to answer your questions, and be thrilled at finding the mouse.

- In each reading pick something from each page to focus on, whether it's the trees or one of the animals. Talk about the animals using color words or other descriptions, such as fluffy ears or tail or beady eyes. Selecting different animals for each reading will make every reread a delight for you and baby.

Counting Kisses
Karen Katz
Board book
Little Simon, 26 pages, 2001

This is a bedtime story that could be read at any time of day because your baby's smiles and body movements will tell you she wants to hear and see the book again and again. With its counting cadence, "Ten little kisses on teeny tiny toes, nine laughing kisses on busy, wriggly feet," and so on, baby experiences parent's loving touch while gazing at the delicious illustrations that feature depictions of family members including mom, dad, sibling, grandma, and pets.

PARENTESE TIPS AND TALKING POINTS ABOUT THE ILLUSTRATIONS:

- The rhyming sounds, along with your playful touches of toes, feet, belly button, etc., will elicit laughter and love from your baby. All you have to do is imitate the physical action depicted in the illustration on each page while you read the rhyme and maintain eye contact with baby. By the time your baby is one year old, she will be able to touch her nose when you say, "touch your nose." These repetitively heard words will be stored for later use.

- You can also point out family members plus the cat and the dog: "Look, here's grandma. Look at her glasses." "What's kitty doing? He's licking the baby's ear."

Clap Hands
Helen Oxenbury
Large board book
Little Simon, 8 pages, 1999
Available in French

Helen Oxenbury's books should be included in every baby and toddler library. *Clap Hands* is one of a series: *All Fall Down, Say Goodnight, and Tickle Tickle*. This series features babies from diverse backgrounds so babies can see other babies who mirror their ethnicity. The illustrations are large and simple, perfect for Stage 2 baby's visual development.

PARENTESE TIPS AND TALKING POINTS ABOUT THE ILLUSTRATIONS:

- When you read this book it may be useful to have your hands free so you can imitate the toddlers' actions that are seen in the illustrations. You'll also want to position baby on a bed or in a car seat so she can see your face and hand movements, as well as the book illustrations. The cadence of the rhythmic chant together with your hand gestures will keep your baby's attention.

- Repeated readings help your baby learn the language structure and eventually the vocabulary. Although you may tire of reading certain books again and again, babies enjoy and need the repetition for brain and language development.

Enséñame Colores
Board book
DK Altea, 18 pages, 2004

This Spanish book is filled with photos that are printed in bold, primary colors. The colors denote categories of objects and animals that are characterized by certain colors. For yellow there are lemons, bananas, sunflowers, a rubber duck, and corn. Each of the items is labeled with a Spanish word.

PARENTESE TIPS AND TALKING POINTS ABOUT THE ILLUSTRATIONS:

Book cover: *Enséñame Colores*

- This book could be used in a number of ways. At this stage, we recommend selecting a picture and describing and talking about it. For example, on the *verde* (green) page, there is a close-up of a green, scaly *lagarto* (lizard). Using your singsongy, parantese voice, you can point out the various features: the big round eye, the five bulbous toes or hands, the bumpy, scaly skin.

- You can ask questions, such as "Where do you think the lizard is going?" Don't forget to look at your baby and wait for a response.

- Follow your baby's lead by talking about the object she may try to reach toward with her closed little fist. As your baby matures, you can start reading the words in Spanish so she can learn the vocabulary.

Animal Crackers, A Delectable Collection of Pictures, Poems, and Lullabies for the Very Young
Jane Dyer
Hardcover
Little, Brown and Company, 62 pages, 1996

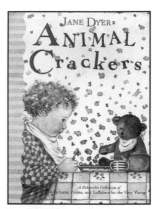

Book cover: *Animal Crackers*

Parents will be drawn to this selection of poems because it includes timeless, traditional English and American rhymes many of us heard growing up: Humpty Dumpty, Wee Willie Winkie, Peter Piper, Hey, Diddle, Diddle, and many more. Poems, rhymes, and songs are grouped according to such themes as ABC, counting, seasons, food, animals, and lullabies. This book is about the rhythm, the rhyme, and the language.

You will notice that some of the poems are long. Your alert observing baby will love a long poem. However, by eighteen months, a toddler might be too active to stay with a longer poem. Yet, if you begin in the early months, these rhymes and poems will become so familiar that your toddler will have many committed to memory. Your baby will enjoy this book all through the preschool and primary school years. The watercolor illustrations by Jane Dyer are so attractive that the adult reader will enjoy the book as much as baby. There are also several board books available using some of the verses from this collection: *Animal Crackers—Nursery Rhymes, Animal Crackers—Bedtime, and Animal Crackers—Animal Friends.*

PARENTESE TIPS AND TALKING POINTS ABOUT THE ILLUSTRATIONS:

- Your emphasis will be on reading the poem all the way through to get the rhythmical flow of the language. Before and after reading the poem, you may look at your baby and say something like, "Now we're going to read a poem about a doggy." When you have finished reading the poem, you may again address your baby by asking a question: "Did you like that poem? Do you want to hear another poem?"

CHAPTER 5

Stage 3: The Cooer

Reading to Your Absorbent Four- to Eight-Month-Old

As you can see everyday, your four- to eight-month-old baby is changing rapidly. You can almost see the growth right before your eyes. He is now becoming a responsive, active member of your family, eagerly searching your face, voice, and actions for information and meaning. Everything your baby hears and sees at this stage will be stored in his brain cells for later use. Amidst all the jumble of sounds in your stream of words, your smart baby can pick out the sounds that represent his name. Babies of only four months recognize their own names, the first word they recognize. This shows how receptive and ready the brain is to learn language right from the start.

Photo by Linda Posnick.

By seven months, babies can understand other words besides their own names. It's good for parents to remember that from this stage onward, babies will understand many more words than they will be able to say. At this phase, nearly every day will bring a revelation of newly acquired skills, such as the ability to grab and hold objects. During these months parents will feel more relaxed as both baby and parents know one another intimately.

If the read-aloud routine has been established, you will note how your baby responds with delight at reading time. Your baby responds to your undivided attention when reading and talking in many ways. Your Cooer will "talk" back to you in a way that will melt your heart. Those coos are full of meaning and love that only a parent can understand. You'll experience the full extent of the baby-parent dialogue or the give-and-take, back-and-forth jabber and coo. Your child is drawing out of you your best parentese voice, full of animation, extended vowel sounds, higher pitched voice, and singsongy rhythm. Locking his gaze onto yours, you're both wrapped in a magical world of loving intimacy through coos, words, and gestures. You realize that you are an extension of your baby's built-in language impulse.[1] You can continue in this dance and lose all sense of time because the experience is so heavenly.

Once a quiescent participant, your teething baby will now reach out and grab the book and may bring it to his mouth. Parents can try reading various book formats—large books with large color photographs or small board books. As your baby reaches eight months, he will become much more active and perhaps distracted if other things are going on around you as you read. Television and loud music or other intruding electronic background noise should be turned off when reading aloud to your baby, so that cooing and dialogue can be encouraged between baby and parent.

Characteristics: Four to Eight Months

Listening

- Prefers parentese to regular speech tone (see Chapter 2). You can gain his attention by changing the pitch, rhythm, and volume of your voice.
- Will listen intently to the sounds and rhythms of language.
- Recognizes own name at four months.
- Can distinguish between the happy, sad, or angry tones of a parent's voice.
- Is able to perceive full range of sounds.
- Likes to hear familiar language repeated, such as a greeting, song, or book.

- Absorbs and memorizes large numbers of sounds and words that will form the foundation of later speech and literacy skills.
- Understands the rhythm and tone of his home language.
- Likes to hear talk about daily routines, such as diaper changing, feeding, and sleeping.
- Can recognize a few words besides own name at seven months.
- Can't discriminate sounds such as mom's reading voice if there is background noise, other loud voices, or television.

Verbal

- At four months, vocalizes when there is eye contact with parent.
- At six or seven months, begins making babbles that sound like language—mamama, dadada.

Visual

- Looks intently at people and objects in immediate environment.
- Continues developing binocular vision and depth perception.
- Can see colors and details clearly.
- Will stare at parent's face and mouth and try to imitate movements.

Motor

- Will reach out to objects that he sees and is able to grasp.
- Is able to sit with support or on his own.
- Can pick up a small object with thumb and forefinger and will often bring it to his mouth.
- Can roll across the floor to pick up an object, such as a small book or toy.
- Likes to examine different features of objects, such as size or texture, and investigate how things work.
- Is interested in cause and effect, such as turning a switch and a light goes on, or pushing a button in a book that generates a sound.

S
T
A
G
E
3

Step-by-Step Read-Aloud Instructions: Four to Eight Months

Select a book from the recommended list at the end of this chapter.

S
T
A
G
E
3

How to position baby: Getting ready

- Hold baby in a sitting position on your lap, or lie on your back beside baby, looking up at the book, or prop him up between your legs on the floor.
- As you read, hold the book so he can clearly see each page.

Parentese interaction

- Embellish the text with questions, extensions, and dramatizations in a way that engages him (see example of mother reading to her eight-month-old twins at this stage).
- Continue reading with an expressive voice, using sound effects for things such as animals, vehicles, and actions. For example, in reading *Barnyard Banter*, dramatize and draw out the animal sounds: *Mooooooo, moooooooo.*
- In order to capitalize on your baby's increasing social interactivity, pause as you read and respond to his babbles and make eye contact. You may even ask questions.
- Remain on each page for only a few seconds or as long as he shows interest.
- When you're reading books with labeled objects and parts of baby anatomy, wait a few seconds to give your baby response time.
- If you are reading a touch-and-feel book, help your baby touch the different textures on each page with his little hand.
- If you are reading a book that involves such baby routines as bathing or feeding, compare or discuss your own baby's routines with ones in the book.
- When reading homemade books, emphasize your baby's name as well as those of close family members.

Photo by Linda Posnick.

Dad reads to baby as three-year-old sister listens.

Challenges

- Baby grabs the book in a way so that you can't read. Allow baby to hold the book if he reaches out for it. Let baby hold that book while you read a different book.

- Teething. If he draws the book to his mouth, allow him to teeth on the book. In the meantime, select another book to read while he teethes on the first book. Sometimes letting him chew on his favorite teething toy keeps him occupied while you talk and read.

- Restlessness. You may find that your baby is more restless at this stage due to teething and the fact that he is more mobile. You may have to change reading positions frequently, or give baby a book to teeth on. Perhaps you'll have to wing it the best you can by only reading a page or so, and mainly talking about what your baby is doing. Just because your baby is active or uncomfortable doesn't mean you should give up on your reading routine. Keep reading!

- Keeping baby's attention. The best way to read under challenging circumstances is to get baby's attention by using your voice at a higher or lower pitch than usual, and dramatizing the words in a way that makes you and your baby smile. For example, it's hard for babies not to stop everything and watch and listen while you call out sounds like caw, caw, hee haw, or cock-a-doodle-doo from *Barnyard Banter* by Denise Fleming. You can extend the fun to later when you are in the middle of feeding or bathing, and then suddenly make some of the animal noises from the book. Notice how your baby perks up and recognizes these now familiar sounds.

- Reading to twins, triplets, or multiple siblings. The mother in the demonstration below is able to read to her twins for a short time. We recommend you try to find a special time to read to each child independently. We know this is difficult. You will have to be determined to set up a routine when both parents are home, and each of you can take a child. Otherwise you will have to alternate while one is napping and playing and the other can be read to.

S
T
A
G
E
3

Read-Aloud Demonstration: Mother Reading to Her Eight-Month-Old Twins

Mom placed her active twin boys in a sitting position on the floor with a book spread out in front of them. She selected a larger format book rather than a small board book so both boys could easily see it. Mom also discovered that larger books are harder for her sons to put in their mouths. One of the striking features of this mom's reading style is her amazing amount of feeling and animation as she interacts with the book and her sons. She is an expert in tailoring her reading style to her twins' needs. For example, she consciously used a variety of voice tones, pitches, and volumes. She tapped her finger on the picture and engaged the more easily distracted twin by saying his name and directing questions to him. This mother is using parentese (see Chapter 2) to actively involve her boys by using dialogue and creating meaning using the book. These babies were premature and were not as verbal or active as a full term eight-month-old. So mother was able to hold their attention in a sitting position for the few minutes of this read-aloud. This read-aloud was less than five minutes.

(Words that are read the way they appear in the book are italicized. All the other words not in italics are mom's own words.)

Look at the book about the animals.
> (Mom's voice is excited as she directs the twin's attention to the cover of the book.)

The Lifesize Animal Counting Book.
Are you ready? AHHHH!
> (Excited voice inhale.)

Look at all the animals! Look at the doggie, just like your doggie? Ahhhhh! Is that like your doggie, little John?
> (Mom slowly stretched out phrase.) (John reaches out to touch doggie.)

The owl and the chicks, and look at the caterpillar!!
> Yeah! Yeah!
> (Mom turns page.)

Oh! Who is this? Ahhh! The gorilla!
> (Mom reads in a louder voice.)

One greedy gorilla. What does the gorilla say?
> (Mom makes gorilla noises.) (Thomas looks at Mom then back at the book.)

Is that what a gorilla says?

(Mom makes gorilla noises.)

That silly gorilla. Is that what he says, Boo, Boo? AHHHH!!
(Loud.)

Two contented cats. What does the kitty say? Meow! Is that what a kitty says? Meow! Meow! See the kitty?

(Mom taps finger audibly on kitty.) (Both twins turn to look at kitty.)

Look, What does the kitty have? See little John, look!

(Mom points.) (Twins look at the balls.)

What does the kitty have? Two little balls, see? The kitty plays with these balls. Let's see what's next . . .

(Mom turns page.)

AHHH!!! LOOK!! The puppies!! What do the puppies say? Ruff, ruff, ruff!

(Deep dog voice.)

Is that what puppies say? OH!! . . . Look!!! at the puppies sleeping. *Three playful puppies.* Want to count the puppies? ONE, TWO, THREE.

(Mom taps finger audibly as she counts the doggies.) (John attempts
to grasp doggies.)

Okay, let's see what's next . . .

(Mom turns page.)

Are you ready? Ohhh!!! Look, we saw these at the zoo! The tortoises! *Four slow tortoises.* Remember, we saw the little tortoises and the big tortoises at the zoo?[2]

What to Notice in the Read-Aloud Demonstration

Notice how the mother:

- Places babies on the floor reading a large book with which they can both interact.
- Does not read text as it appears: Mom interjects her own words related to book text.
- Adjusts the text to the toddlers. She also speaks in parentese by using an excited, animated voice that sometimes pauses, slows down, or increases in volume to capture the twins' attention.
- Uses a different tone of voice when reading the text directly out of the book.

S
T
A
G
E
3

- Is extremely animated and speaks in a fast pace to keep the twins' attention.
- Engages in questioning even though the boys cannot yet verbalize answers.
- Makes animal noises to keep babies interested.
- Taps fingers loudly on book as she counts the doggies. This helps keep the boys focused on the book.
- Asks questions and allows waiting time so that the boys can respond with an excited breath, a coo, or grunt.
- Follows the boys' lead by asking questions based on the picture they are touching.
- Says the name of the baby that seems to be the most distracted as she talks about the book. This helps him stay focused.
- Relates the book to their own life experiences. "Look at the doggie, just like your doggie."
- Uses descriptive words and expands on the vocabulary in the text by relating it to their life experiences. "Remember, we saw the little tortoises and the big tortoises at the zoo?"
- Reads a book appropriate for this stage and her particular situation reading with twins. The book she selects is a larger-scale book with realistic pictures of animals.
- Uses the book's topics to teach concepts such as counting, animal names, and sounds.

See "Baby Book Reviews at a Glance" for more ideas on what to talk about when reading this book and others.

Characteristics of Stage 3 Books

Books for this stage need to cover a lot of ground. They need to introduce basic vocabulary that is related to baby's environment and experience. Hearing lots of words is important at this time, since your baby's brain is storing words in his memory bank. Books that discuss a typical set of baby routines, like bath time, eating, and bedtime, will help him hear vocabulary labels for each activity.

Four- to eight-month-old babies also are attracted to books with textures and flaps for sensory exploration. Now that baby is beginning to grasp, he will appreciate exploring the sense of touch. All your baby's senses are awakened. Your baby is more and more tuned into illustrations because of improving visual skills. Choose books that stimulate a range of senses.

Mini board books are tiny little books that feature illustrated objects with one or two word labels. They measure about three inches square, and easily fit into little hands. Mini books are like little toy books, but some have exceptionally good quality, such as the DK series. It's a delight to see your eight- or nine-month-old sitting on the floor holding a mini board book, turning the pages just like an older child.

In our age of computers and digital photographs, it's easy to create some of your own baby books with family photos and pictures of your baby involved in all his routines, including participating in read-alouds and special occasions. A homemade book, if laminated to protect it from rough treatment including teething, can be kept for many years as a family memento. (See Chapter 12 for more ideas on homemade books.)

Recommended Types of Books: Four to Eight Months

- Homemade books with faces of family members and friends or pets
- Mini board books that baby can easily hold and turn the pages
- Rhyming books
- Books with words and pictures about routines such as bathing, eating, and sleeping
- Old books or magazines that the baby can hold, manipulate, and tear
- Touch-and-feel books that stimulate senses
- Large books with colorful pictures and sturdy pages
- Plastic or cloth books that can be used in the bathtub or put in mouth (teething books)
- Books that label objects, toys, or parts of the body
- Books with illustrations well matched to the text

Baby Book Reviews at a Glance

Pat the Bunny, Let's Find Bunny
Inspired by original *Pat the Bunny* by Dorothy Kunhardt
Board book

Golden Books, 10 pages, 1999
Available in French

This is a touch-and-feel book that babies at four to eight months love to grasp for the different sensations of textures of cloth. In addition, babies enjoy the suspenseful dialogue as you search for the bunny. This is the same hide-and-seek game you'll play with your baby and toddler under the blankets or behind a chair. The drawings are simple, with touches of color to make it easy to identify each object. Your baby is sure to enjoy this and other *Pat the Bunny* books, inspired by the original *Pat the Bunny* by Dorothy Kunhardt, one of the best-loved baby books of all time.

PARENTESE TIPS AND TALKING POINTS ABOUT THE ILLUSTRATIONS:

- By eight months, babies are beginning to know many words that they can't yet express. You can read the book as is, or you can point to common items and name them: chair, curtain, table, door, bathtub. Pointing and naming helps reinforce your baby's vocabulary development. Soon your baby will be able to point to the chair when you ask, "Where is the chair?"

- When you ask your baby to find what's under the flap, emphasize the concepts of under, behind, and in, as you answer your own question for your baby, modeling the correct language. "Where is the kitty? Oh look, the kitty is under the quilt."

Bedtime, a Razzle Dazzle Book
Chuck Murphy
Board book
Little Simon, 10 pages, 1998
Available in French

Here is a visually stimulating book that features a variety of glistening bright surfaces. The small size is easy to handle. The bedtime theme will help your baby make the transition to sleep. Each illustration has a one- or two-word caption. The most important feature of this book is the visual appeal of the glittery, shiny material in each illustration.

PARENTESE TIPS AND TALKING POINTS ABOUT THE ILLUSTRATIONS:

- Although there are only one or two words on each page, you'll find plenty to talk about in this book. For example, the illustration of the boy taking a bath can be used to discuss your baby's bath routine. You can say, "Look at the boy taking a bath, playing with his boat. Let's count the bubbles, one, two, three, and look at the shimmering water. Can you find the soap?"

- You can ask your baby to find and point to the shiny objects on each page. "Where is the shiny water? Where is the sparkly duck? Where is the shimmering moon?" Your baby will learn a variety of descriptive words for the glittering objects.

Night-Night Baby, a Touch-and-Feel Book
Elizabeth Hathon, photographer
Board book
Grosset & Dunlap, 12 pages, 2000

Touch-and-feel books have their place in a baby's library. *Night-Night Baby* has a shiny plastic duck, a fluffy rug, a mirror, and cotton curtains for baby to explore. The full-page photographs showing babies of different ethnicities in the bath or in the high chair will hold your baby's attention page after page.

PARENTESE TIPS AND TALKING POINTS ABOUT THE ILLUSTRATIONS:

- You can read the words in the book or make up your own words based on baby's home routine. For example, there is a nice photograph of a father reading to his baby. The book they are looking at is a flap that opens like a real book. The miniature book has a photograph of a baby on both the cover and the inside. You can say, "Look, this baby is reading like we read. Let's see what he's reading about. Look, there's a smiling baby with his soft teddy bear."

- Each photograph depicts a routine in baby's day. Talk about how your baby eats or drinks, bathes, or gets ready for bed. Always relate your own baby's experiences to those in the books you read.

My Very First Word Book
Angela Wilkes
Hardcover
Dorling Kindersley Publishing, 21 pages, 1993
Available in Spanish and French

My Very First Word Book is organized in themes, from home items to animals and things that go. The photographs of everyday objects in your baby's environment will give parents ideas of vocabulary to practice with your baby. The pictures are simple, bright, and colorful—perfect for pointing to and naming. There is even an index, which includes the numerous objects pictured in the book.

PARENTESE TIPS AND TALKING POINTS ABOUT THE ILLUSTRATIONS:

- By naming the objects as you point to the bright, clear photographs, you help your baby store these names in his brain. When he is ready, he will point to or name each item himself. You don't have to name all the pictures in one sitting, but select themes your baby can relate to now.

- You can talk about just one page, the "all about me" page. You can look at the nose in the picture and then touch your baby's nose. One of the first words babies say is *nose* or *eyes*.

- As your baby matures, talk about shapes, colors, patterns, and numbers.

Fish Eyes: A Book You Can Count On
Lois Ehlert
Paperback, Board book
Red Wagon Books/Harcourt, 38
    pages, 1990

Book cover: *Fish Eyes*

Lois Ehlert, the author and illustrator of many lively books for children, created this colorful, boldly designed book filled with patterned fish, some with cutout eyes revealing the colors on the next page. Starting with a few pages of simple rhymes, the book continues counting from "one green fish" to "ten darting fish." At four to eight months, your baby's eyes are beginning to see three-dimensional images. The brilliantly colored fish will hold your baby's attention as you read and embellish the text, tailoring it to your baby.

PARENTESE TIPS AND TALKING POINTS ABOUT THE ILLUSTRATIONS:

- Try reading the rhymes in the first eight pages of the book as they are written. When you start the counting section, use the author's adjectives when you talk to your baby about the fish. For example, if you don't read "5 spotted fish" straight from the text, use "spotted" when you talk to your baby about the fish. Say something like, "Look at the spots. See the green spots and the blue spots? The fish are spotted."

- There are some imaginative adjective words used to describe fish that, when heard repeatedly, will eventually become part of your child's vocabulary. Also try making up your own adjectives to describe the fish, such as fast, sleepy, and hungry.

Happy Baby, It's My Day
Board book
Pride Bicknell, 10 pages, 2001

Part of the *Happy Baby* series, *It's My Day* features ten board pages, each with a photograph of a smiling baby involved in daily activities. The book is shaped like a baby's head with a visible mirror on each page, including the cover—a feature that will attract your baby's attention from the start.

PARENTESE TIPS AND TALKING POINTS ABOUT THE ILLUSTRATIONS:

- Talk about the photos of a baby hand and foot or the baby toys. Ask the questions on each page. At this age babies will not yet be able to verbally answer, but parents can answer for them, modeling the question-and-answer process. For example, you might say, "Can you find your toes?" Walk your fingers down your baby's leg, and say, "Oh look, your toes are at the end of your foot, one, two, three, four, five yummy toes."

- Put the mirror from the book in front of your baby's face and ask him to point to his nose or eyes. Then have him point to the nose and eyes of each baby in the book.

The Lifesize Animal Counting Book
Editor, Jinn von Noreen, Designer, Ingrid Mason
Large Hardcover
Dorling Kindersley Publishing, 30 pages, 1994

This is the book used in the demonstration of the mother reading to her twins earlier in this chapter. The fact that this is a simple counting book is incidental at this stage. What's important is the amount of "dialogue" generated from the engaging large photos of animals and insects that are truly life-size. The book starts with one gorilla, and after the number 10, the numbers skip to "20 butterflies", and "100 creepy crawlers." The photographs are eye-catching for any age.

Book cover: *The Lifesize Animal Counting Book*

**PARENTESE TIPS AND TALKING POINTS
ABOUT THE ILLUSTRATIONS:**

- At this stage, your baby will recognize most of the animals because they are pets: cats, kittens, puppies, rabbits, and guinea pigs. The photos are so appealing and realistic that you want to touch them. Ask your baby, "Where are the doggies?" Notice how your baby responds to your questions.

- You don't have to start at the beginning, and you may not finish the book because you might have so much to say about just one or two pictures. Skip around to your baby's favorite pages.

- In the example of the mother reading, note how mother tapped audibly on the pictures. You could do this when you count. For example, "Three playful puppies," and then tap as you count 1, 2, 3. This helps baby focus on the book.

Barnyard Banter
Denise Fleming
Board book
Henry Holt and Company, 28 pages, 1997

Barnyard Banter is just what the title says: a lot of bantering noise. This small book might become the favorite of your four- to eight-month-old because of the fun, noisy way you interpret the animal sounds.

PARENTESE TIPS AND TALKING POINTS ABOUT THE ILLUSTRATIONS:

- Few babies can resist your funny voice dramatizations of animal sounds such as "moo, moo, moo" in a deep voice. Or "cock-a-doodle-doo" in your high-pitched, best rooster imitation voice. Even if your baby is agitated or feeling discomfort for some reason, he'll suddenly turn toward you with an intent look of concentration, and probably smile when you really ham it up. Neither you nor your baby will tire of this kind of fun.

- Another way of reading this book is to sing the verses to the tune of *Skip to My Lou,* still dramatizing the sounds of the animals.

- In a few months your baby will be babbling "moo, moo, moo" for a cow as you read this book aloud. *Barnyard Banter* will help prepare him for the next stages, so that by the time he becomes a toddler, and after dozens of readings, he'll have all the animal sounds memorized. But this is no ordinary rhyming list of animal sounds. There is a mystery. "Where is the goose? Is she hiding? Can you see her?" Baby will delight in the question and in the search for the goose that can be found on every bright-colored page.

Whose Back Is Bumpy?
Kate Davis, illustrated by Bob Filipowich
A nontoxic, soft plastic textured board book
Innovative Kids, 8 pages, 2000

A variation on a lift-up flap book, *Whose Back Is Bumpy?* has five thick, soft-to-the-touch, plastic "pages" with puzzle-like lift-out textured animals. Unlike some specialty cloth or plastic books, *Whose Back is Bumpy?* has interesting vocabulary and asks a question on each page. A book that can withstand teething as well as the bathtub, your child will later use the removable animal pieces as puzzles. It would also make a good shower gift, as it is part toy and part book. There are other books in this series: *In and Out, Big and Little, Colors, Seasons, My Ducky, Shapes*, and several more.

PARENTESE TIPS AND TALKING POINTS ABOUT THE ILLUSTRATIONS:

- As you read the book to your baby, let him hold one of the animal pieces and teeth on it. At four to eight months, your baby is beginning to reach out and grab objects in order to investigate their sensory qualities. He'll want to put the object in his mouth.

- Read the rhyme, and then when you ask the question about how the animal feels, hold your baby's hand and rub it against the texture of the animal piece.

¿Dónde está el ombliguito?
Karen Katz
Board book
Simon and Schuster Libros Para Niños, 12 pages, 2004

This is another play on peek-a-boo as mom looks for baby's eyes, mouth, and so on. The wording is very natural using the diminutive (ojos/ojitos, eyes/little eyes) form that is commonly used when Spanish-speaking parents talk to their babies. It's parentese Spanish style! This is not a bilingual book. However, the book is also available in English along with other books by Karen Katz: *Grandma and Me* and *Where Is Baby's Mommy?* All the illustrations are bright and warm, full of loving, cuddly family members.

PARENTESE TIPS AND TALKING POINTS ABOUT THE ILLUSTRATIONS:

- Read the question and help baby open the flap to find the part of the body or face named in the question. Act surprised as the flap opens revealing the part that the baby in the illustration points to.

- First you look for the baby's eyes, etc., in the book, and then you could sit in front of a mirror and ask the same questions as in the book and have baby point to his own eyes.

- Besides answering the questions, discuss the things in the illustration that your baby can relate to, such as the animals and the toys.

CHAPTER 6

Stage 4: The Babbler

Reading to Your Vocal Eight- to Twelve-Month-Old

Reading to your baby at this stage is a total delight. Here's why. At this time the many benefits of all the reading aloud you've done since birth will become apparent. You'll see how much your baby has developed a love and understanding of books by the way she can sit by her box of favorite books and look at them independently with no help from her parents. She is capable of sitting, turning pages, and studying for many minutes at a time the books that you've read repeatedly. You may even catch her smiling or laughing at her favorite illustrations.

What's more, she knows what her favorite books are about, because when you make an animal sound the way you do when you read *Barnyard Banter*, for example, she will look at her book box, crawl over to it, and take out *Barnyard Banter*. This is something you can try with the books you have read, especially after ten months of age. Repeat a phrase from one of her favorite books, make an animal sound, or simply ask her where her favorite

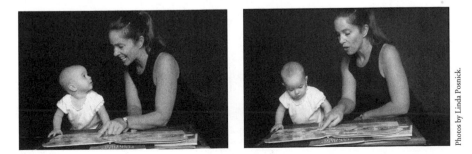

S
T
A
G
E

4

Photos by Linda Posnick.

95

character is, and you will marvel at her ability to crawl over and select the correct book. Try this with some of the books you have read over and over, to verify how receptive your baby has been to your daily reading.

In addition to her increased attention span, in Stage 4 your baby's vision is almost as mature as adult vision. Not only can she now enjoy the color and detail of the illustrations, she can understand a lot of words. You have probably noticed that when she hears words like mommy, daddy, truck, or bird, she looks in the direction of the person or object. She knows these and other words because you have repeated them daily when reading and talking.

Because she has been read to since birth, she will now sit on your lap and listen and look with concentrated interest at the book, as she turns pages. She even knows how to wait to turn the page until you are finished reading or talking about it. When you point at an object on the page, she looks where you are pointing. If you point to a dog and go "wuff-wuff," she expects you to make that same barking sound each time you read that book. When she begins speaking, she will say, "wuff, wuff."

As the name, "the Babbler," for this stage implies, you'll notice that your baby can say most of the sounds. You'll hear "da" and "gu" and "ba" and all kinds of variations. Your baby will hold up her end of the conversation by gesturing, pointing, and babbling during your daily read-alouds. You, in turn, should listen and respond like you understand every word she says. Parents are so tuned in to their baby's code that they often understand what baby's sounds mean. Babies have ways of letting you know their needs.

Babbling of sounds is a crucial milestone on the literacy journey. The skill of babbling—and it truly is a skill—is the result of having heard your slowed, high-pitch, directed parentese speech since birth. As babies babble they are learning how to distinguish individual sounds in words. This distinguishing of individual sounds in the stream of speech, called *phonemic awareness*, is tested at kindergarten and is a strong predictor of success in reading. Being able to hear and distinguish the smallest units of speech leads to letter sound recognition and is an important part of reading and writing. Your babbler is on her way to becoming a successful reader, and she is just about to complete her first year of life.[1]

Characteristics: Eight to Twelve Months

Listening

• You can gain her attention by changing the pitch, rhythm, and volume of your voice. Prefers parentese to regular speech tone (see Chapter 2).

- Begins to understand a number of meanings of words around nine months of age.
- Understands, but cannot yet say, an average of fifty words at twelve months.
- Understands the meaning of "no."
- Understands various action words.
- Understands words that are part of her daily routine, such as eating, bath time, changing clothes, and diapers.
- Absorbs words and reserves them in memory for later use.
- Is developing ability to remember language that is heard repetitively from books or experiences with parents.
- Can listen with full attention when background noise is reduced and television is turned off.

Verbal

- Can make most speech sounds.
- Is beginning to make words at ten months, but will continue to babble beyond first year.
- Dialogues by gesturing, pointing, and talking. (Example: waves bye-bye and claps.)
- Produces sounds that objects (airplanes and cars) and animals make instead of the words for objects and animals. For example, "*wuff, wuff*" for dog.

Visual

- Has fully developed color, detail, and visual depth perception.
- Looks at objects parent points to rather than at parent's finger.

Motor

- Discovers self in mirror and photographs.
- Crawls, climbs, stands unassisted, and walks with help. Can crawl to the bookcase and pull out books.
- Has increasing control of hand movements. Indication of hand dominance.
- Turns pages and points to pictures as you read.
- Likes to examine different features of objects, such as size, texture, and how things work. (Example: at this stage, babies are wild about books with flaps and gimmicks.)

S
T
A
G
E
4

Step-by-Step Read-Aloud Instructions: Eight to Twelve Months

Select a book from the recommended list at the end of this chapter.

How to position baby: Getting ready

- Since your baby can sit on her own and probably crawl, select any reading position that you both find comfortable. Sometimes placing your baby on your lap or lying down on your backs works well, since it keeps her from moving around.
- Whatever position you choose, make sure your baby can see the illustrations. Point to them and encourage baby to interact with any textures, flaps, or buttons.

Parentese interaction

Photo by Linda Posnick.

In a standing position leaning against a table, baby lifts and opens flap with her finger.

- Continue reading or conversing with an expressive voice, using sound effects for things such as animals, vehicles, and actions. For example, reading *Where's Spot?* dramatize questions such as "Is Spot in the piano?" Change the tone of your voice and shake your head when saying "NO" for each animal. Your one-year-old may shake her head when you say "NO." She may also say "wuff-wuff" when she sees Spot.
- To encourage your baby's increasing social interactivity, pause as you read and after asking questions. Respond to your baby's babbles and make eye contact.
- Reread favorite books. Books like *Where's Spot?* can be read again and again, thus helping your baby learn to say the word *NO*. Other words such as *inside* and *under* will be learned and reserved in memory to be verbalized later.
- Continue reading some of the favorite books from previous stages. Notice how your baby attempts to say some of the familiar sounds or words. Babies will anticipate a favorite part of the book. If you usually

S
T
A
G
E
4

make a particular sound when you see an animal in a book, your baby will anticipate and expect you to make that sound at each reading. She will get excited with anticipation and maybe try to make the sound herself.

Challenges

- Since baby is so mobile, you may have to adjust your position to accommodate her perhaps several times during a reading session. For example, if you start your reading session with your baby sitting on your lap on the carpet, you could end up on your backs reading, or baby might stand supported by an ottoman or coffee table, as you switch back and forth between books.

- Baby may look at book and then at toys or something else in environment, and then back at book illustrations. Just keep reading. If you read with enough excitement you will gain baby's attention through most of the book.

- Some babies are very strong, and if they grab the flaps on interactive books just right, they can rip them off. This can be tricky. Find a way of turning pages and flipping flaps so baby can touch and be a participant, yet not totally destroy the book. If you're not comfortable with a book being ripped, you might want to wait to introduce flap books until the baby is older and has better hand coordination. Babies should not be scolded if a page in a book is ripped. They are too young to understand, and don't yet have the hand coordination. Assume that some of the pages in your baby books will get ripped eventually.

- Bringing books to baby's mouth is one more means of sensory exploration. Allow baby to grab, hold, and bring book to her mouth. If you don't want baby to teeth on a book, give her a teether book (cloth books with rubber edges of different textures). Many babies have chewed the corners off favorite books and suffered no adverse affects. The books may appear a little worse for wear, but can still be read and enjoyed. Baby books published in the United States are made of nontoxic materials.

Read-Aloud Demonstration: Mother Reading to Her Twelve-Month-Old

During this special reading time Mom is interacting and talking with Olivia in a way that assumes that Olivia is understanding everything she says. At around twelve months, babies understand many more words than they can actually say. At this point, Olivia is still mostly babbling, but she points to all the objects and illustrations that Mom discusses.

Except for the first few pages, there is no text, just illustrations that tell a story. Mom makes up the story in her own words. She asks many questions, while Olivia answers with babbles and finger pointing. When Olivia points to something, Mom talks about it. Mom gives positive feedback ("That's right!") in response to Olivia's babbles.

(Words that are read the way they appear in the book are italicized. All the other words not in italics are mom's own words.)

That's Carl. (Mom says as Olivia points to the dog on the cover.)

Carl's Afternoon in the Park. Here is Carl with the puppy. They are surrounded by flowers and grass. They are in the park. Who is this?

(Olivia babbles.)

That's right; that's the baby. *What a surprise to see you here, Sarah! Let's go have some tea.* She ran into her friend and said let's go have some tea, friend. The friend said fine. Carl is such a good dog, he is going to take care of the baby. What does baby do? She gets up on top of Carl. Oh! Look where they are going! To the carousel. Wow! What's this?

(Olivia babbles.)

A chicken, and what's that?

(Olivia babbles.)

A horse. There are different animals in the carousel. Now they are going to the flower garden. Oh, Oh! Look at the puppy. What is puppy doing? He is playing with the hose. And what is baby doing? He is playing with the flowers. They are having fun in the flower garden?

(Olivia babbles.)

That's right. Look at all these flowers. There are orange ones and pink ones and white ones and purple flowers.

(Olivia babbles.)

That's right. He has the hose in his mouth. I hope he does not rip the hose with those sharp teeth of his. Oh! What are they doing? They are playing with the water. Oh! Look at that! They are shaking it all off.

Now they found the balloon lady. What does the doggie have? What is this?

>   (Mom points to a balloon.) (Olivia babbles.)

A balloon! He has a blue balloon. And what does the baby have?

>   (Olivia babbles.)

A red balloon. Do you think Carl made that doggie balloon? Or do you think Carl got the balloon for her? Oh! Look at that. They are on the train. Choo! Choo! Choo! Look, this train goes around the park.

>   (Mom slides her finger in a circular motion.)

That looks like fun! Now they are at the children's zoo. What are you pointing to? That's the sheep, baa, baa. Where is the pig? Do you see the pig?

>   (Olivia points to the pig.)

That's right. Look at the chubby pig

>   (Olivia babbles as she points to the dog.)

That's the doggie.

>   (Mom continued this type of interaction for the remainder of the book.)[2]

What to Notice in the Read-Aloud Demonstration

Notice how the mother:

- Sits with baby on her lap so that both mom and baby can look and point to illustrations.

- Interjects her own words related to the illustrations in this mostly wordless book.

- Adjusts the text to the toddler. She also speaks in parentese by using an excited, animated voice that sometimes pauses, slows down, or increases in volume to capture Olivia's attention.

- Engages in conversation throughout the book, constantly questioning Olivia and pulling her into the conversation.

- Helps Olivia learn the names of things by asking "What's that?", allowing response time; after Olivia's babble, responds to the question, "That's right, it's a chicken."

S
T
A
G
E

4

- Acknowledges Olivia's babbles in a positive way, encouraging her participation. Mom responds to one of Olivia's babbles, "That's right, he has a hose in his mouth."

- Teaches concepts such as colors.

- Follows Olivia's lead by asking questions based on the picture she is pointing to.

- Is able to follow the story plot from beginning to end in a sequential order. Again Mom was following Olivia's lead as she was interested in following the storyline. Other babies might like to skip around from page to page, just talking about what they see on each page but not following the story in the book.

- Reads a book based on her daughter's specific interests—puppies and, based on Olivia's daily experiences, visiting parks.

- Uses the book's topics to teach concepts such as colors, animal names, and sounds. Introduces new words by describing the park setting.

- Asks Olivia to predict what will happen in the story.

See "Baby Book Reviews at a Glance" below for more ideas on what to talk about when reading this book and others.

Characteristics of Stage 4 Books

These are the few months just before talking begins. Your baby is building a reservoir of words that, when you first hear them, will be cause for great celebration. The repeated words from every book you read will go straight into this reservoir. Some of the books we've selected can be sung, like Raffi's *Wheels on the Bus*. Others, like Eric Hill's *Where's Spot?*, have features such as hidden animals behind flaps that prompt baby to say "no" in answer to questions. At this stage you can read books with more complicated illustrations that encourage talking, pointing, and looking for details.

Babies are beginning to show their unique interests, and parents are guided to select books that reflect these interests, such as zoo animals, construction vehicles, ballerinas, or princesses. Parents can find board books that have either illustrations or action words like running and jumping, and concepts like under, over, inside, and outside.

Parents can celebrate baby's first birthday with a homemade book of photographs of baby since birth with friends and relatives. You can choose to label photos, or even create your own rhyme, or just include photos to talk about. Baby will enjoy going back to a homemade book over and over and hearing about family members. (See more ideas on homemade books in Chapter 12.) Most of the books for this stage support your baby's rapidly escalating vocabulary of words that she is now beginning to understand, and will soon be able to say.

Recommended Types of Books: Eight to Twelve Months

- Books with accompanying CDs and tapes by artists such as Raffi, with favorite children's songs like "The Wheels on the Bus" and "Old McDonald Had a Farm" and many other favorites that have repetitive choruses
- Homemade books about baby's first birthday or other experiences
- Rhyming books
- Books that label objects, toys, or parts of the body
- Books reflecting baby's daily experiences, such as animals at the zoo, construction site vehicles, or shopping with parents
- Specialty books with different shapes, textures, and sizes, with mirrors or noise buttons
- Books exploring space and time concepts, such as inside, under, after, and next
- Books illustrating action words, such as running, jumping, or sliding
- Books that encourage children to chime in and repeat a word or phrase

S
T
A
G
E
4

Baby Book Reviews at a Glance

Rain Dance
Kathi Appelt, illustrated by Emilie Chollat
Hardcover
Harper Festival, 20 pages, 2001

A book filled with fanciful action vocabulary, *Rain Dance* describes what animals do when it rains. The simple, bold illustrations echo the brevity of the rhymes "2 Spiders Skitter," and so on. This book is part of the *Harper Growing Tree* series, which on the back cover gives parents helpful tips on how to share the book with their child.

PARENTESE TIPS AND TALKING POINTS ABOUT THE ILLUSTRATIONS:

- Parents can make movements with their hands to help baby absorb and eventually understand the action words that add to the fun.

- After parent has repetitively read and partially memorized the easy two words per text page, recite some of the fun phrases during the day when you encounter any of the book's creatures.

Good Night, Gorilla
Peggy Rathmann
Board book
G.P. Putnam's Sons, 34 pages, 1994
Available in Spanish and French

If we had to list our top ten favorite baby books, *Good Night, Gorilla* would be at the top of the list. We saw a premature baby being read this book while in the NICU (Neonatal Intensive Care Unit) for two months. It continued to be one of this child's favorite books for the next two years. The story, which only uses the words *"good night"* and the names of the zoo animals, is mainly wordless. It shows the gorilla furtively lifting the keys from the zookeeper's belt and unlocking all the cages. The animals follow the zookeeper into his bedroom. The zookeeper's wife awakens and takes them all back to the zoo, but the clever gorilla escapes undetected and sneaks into bed again with his pal, the mouse.

- Babies in the eight- to twelve-month range are attracted to the pages with white on black "Good Night" repeated a number of times in different sizes. When parents read each size "Good Night" in a different voice, from deep low sounds to little squeaky sounds, it amuses and holds baby's attention. Your baby, though not yet saying "Good Night" clearly, will soon point and imitate your tones, a step in learning to say these words correctly.

- There are many elements for babies and toddlers to revel in. The illustrations are colorful, funny, and simple. There are opportunities for conversation, such as "Look, the gorilla is using the blue key to open the lion's blue cage." You can also ask questions: "What's that animal? Where's the mouse?"

- Your baby will look and respond to your exaggerated animal sounds. At this stage, your baby will comprehend when you point and say the animal names. Soon, she'll answer by pointing, and then later, verbally answer your questions. Each reading will foster a new creative voice that will hold your baby's interest.

STAGE 4

Goodnight Moon
Margaret Wise Brown, illustrated by Clement Hurd
Paperback
Harper Trophy, 30 pages, 1975
Available in Spanish and French

A little rabbit in bed says "Goodnight" to everything around him as his room gets darker and darker. This classic is loved by parents and babies everywhere. We know of bilingual children who have heard it repeatedly in Spanish (*Buenas Noches Luna*) from six months to five years. The repetitive goodnight, and the naming of simple objects one after the other, holds baby's attention.

Some of the magical illustrations are gray or black and white and some are vivid primary colors. The drawings have a miniature doll-house look endearing to babies.

- Name and point to zoo animals and objects and follow the tiny mouse throughout the book. Ask, "Can you find the mouse?"

- There are lots of opportunities for "conversation" between you and your baby as you talk about the objects and creatures on each page. At around nine to twelve months, your baby knows many more words than she can say. When you ask of the whereabouts of objects in the room, she knows what you mean and soon will be able to name them, and can probably already point to them.

Wheels on the Bus, Songs to Read
Raffi, illustrated by Sylvie Kantorovitz
Board book
Random House, 26 pages, 1988

A playful book whose familiar tune you can sing while looking at the adorable illustrations. The CD or cassette version by Raffi is also available through Troubadour Records. We recommend CDs or cassettes by Raffi, as they are very appropriate for babies, toddlers, and kindergartners. You will notice how intensely your baby will listen to Raffi's easy-to-listen-to voice. His voice is pleasing to adults as well as children. There are other board books in the Raffi series, such as *Baby Beluga*.

PARENTESE TIPS AND TALKING POINTS ABOUT THE ILLUSTRATIONS:

- If you are not familiar with the tune, it's included on the last page so you can try it on the piano or other instruments. The rhythmical, repetitive stanzas demand to be sung or chanted. While singing, you can make rotating motions with babies' hands when you sing or read about the wheels going round and round. Then you can make your arm go back and forth to the rhythm of the swish, swish, swish of the wipers. You may not sound like Raffi, but your baby will prefer your voice and your attention over that of any other.

- The illustrations are a treasure trove of information to be discussed on different levels, depending on the age and stage of your baby. What's fun is that among the bus load of people is the baby who goes "wah wah wah." Babies love hearing you dramatize the "wah wah wah" as they look at the crying baby. They'll also be interested in the illustrations of children, animals, and all the other characters on the bus.

S
T
A
G
E
4

Where's Spot?
Eric Hill
Board book
G.P. Putnam's Sons, 20 pages, 2000
Available in Spanish and French

There are a series of *Spot* books by Eric Hill, but our favorite for babies is *Where's Spot?* Kindergartners and first graders also enjoy *Where's Spot?* because of the universal appeal of the peek-a-boo theme. *Where's Spot?* is about a mother dog and her puppy, Spot. The mother dog looks for Spot. This book is universal because it's the game all parents play with babies when you cover them with a blanket and ask, "Where's baby?"

PARENTESE TIPS AND TALKING POINTS ABOUT THE ILLUSTRATIONS:

- The text asks, "Is he behind the door?" and baby, with parent's help, can open the flap door to reveal a monkey who says, "No." Then Spot's mother looks inside the clock and so on, until she finally finds him in a basket. As soon as you finish reading, you will be asked to read again. Your baby will want to say "No" (or shake her head back and forth) as each flap opens. Soon your baby might be repeating some or part of the questions, too.

- This book also features concepts such as behind, inside, in, and under. When you're reading, before you open the flap, emphasize these words by slowing your speech, raising your volume, and pausing a moment before continuing with the rest of the question. Indicate the movements with your hand or by moving the book up or down.

Best First Book Ever!
Richard Scarry
Hardcover
Random House, 46 pages, 1979
Available in Spanish

You probably remember the Richard Scarry books from when you were a child. Children love his unique style of intricate details and animal characters that dress up like people and go about the day in their strange vehicles.

S
T
A
G
E
4

Many books by Richard Scarry have been translated into French and Spanish.

In *Best First Book Ever!* Scarry's familiar characters, Huckle Cat and Lowly Worm, help with the housework, go to school, play in the playground, shop at the supermarket, visit the doctor, look at a farm, drive to the harbor, and stop at the railroad station.

PARENTESE TIPS AND TALKING POINTS ABOUT THE ILLUSTRATIONS:

- This book provides endless opportunities for practicing words with your baby: colors, parts of the body, clothing, vehicles, household objects, and the alphabet. It even includes Mother Goose rhymes.

- This is an opportunity for parents to relate the pictures and words in the book to baby's own experiences. For example, after reading about Huckle Cat's visit to the doctor, you could say something like, "When you went to the doctor, she listened to your heart with a stethoscope just like Huckle Cat (touching your baby's heart area)."

- When talking about the pictures in the book, emphasize unusual words like stethoscope (pointing to it in the illustration) to expand your child's vocabulary. Children will learn any word as long as it's repeated enough and they understand its meaning.

Freight Train
Donald Crews
Board book
Harper Festival, 20 pages, 1978

This beautifully designed, award-winning book begins with two or three large freight cars of different colors. The simple text (the color of which matches the color of the freight car) names the kind of car and color. Eventually we see the entire train as it moves along and is gone, trailing smoke behind it. Another favorite vehicle book by Crews is *Truck*. Even the youngest toddlers enjoy these vehicle books, both Caldecott Honor Books.

PARENTESE TIPS AND TALKING POINTS ABOUT THE ILLUSTRATIONS:

- The way you read this book will determine how much your baby likes it. At the beginning, you'll start out naming the freight cars and colors.

The central two pages of the book show the entire train with smoke coming from the engine. Babies love smoke, and it may be one of their first words.

- As the train starts picking up speed, and illustrations depict a blurred train, parent can make increasingly fast chug, chug, chug, choo, choo, choo sounds and intermittent toot, toots. It gets suspenseful all the way to the last page that says, "gone." In addition, to help your baby understand the blur of an image caused by speed, move your hand fast back and forth. Maybe at the end your baby will make hand movements that mean "all gone."

Bubbles, Bubbles
Kathi Appelt, illustrated by Fumi Kosaka
Hardcover
Harper Festival, 20 pages, 2001

Filled with whimsical words, *Bubbles, Bubbles* will add to your toddler's rapidly growing vocabulary. Fascinating words like waterlogged, disappeared, glimmer, and glitter will delight your baby's ears.

PARENTESE TIPS AND TALKING POINTS ABOUT THE ILLUSTRATIONS:

- The swift cadence of the rhyme can be chanted when your baby is in the bath. Toddlers scream with delight when a parent touches the tummy, knees, or tootsies mentioned. Toddlers particularly like the humorous illustration of the girl with her hair stiff with pasty, bubbly shampoo. Getting out of the bath is as fun as getting in when baby hears, "Give a shimmy, give a shake, bring a towel, for goodness sake."

- Try to read at least one page of text before you talk about the illustrations. Then you can talk about the names of the different items of clothing she takes off, the toys she brings to the tub, how she scrubs and plays with bubbles, and how she waves good-bye to dirt.

S
T
A
G
E
4

Peek-a-Moo
Marie Torres Cimarusti, illustrated by Stephanie Peterson
Hardcover
Dutton Children's Books, 10 pages, 1998

Who's in the barnyard playing peek-a-boo? This is a perfect book for your 8- to 12-month-old who not only loves pulling down the sturdy flaps, but also is learning to identify animals by their sounds. The illustrations are bold, graphic depictions on plain, vividly colored backgrounds featuring the following: a cow, a pig, a mouse, an owl, a rooster, a sheep, a duck, and finally the peek-a-boo you.

PARENTESE TIPS AND TALKING POINTS ABOUT THE ILLUSTRATIONS:

- Read the text, and when you ask the question, slow down your voice, making it suspenseful. Pause as you open the flap quickly. Raise your voice and read what's under the flap in a surprised voice.

- You can name the animals and show your baby how to point to the eyes, ears, beak, nostrils, hooves, wings, and other parts of the body.

- Then you can play your own peek-a-boo game with your baby.

Carl's Afternoon in the Park
Alexandra Day
Board book
Farrar, Straus, Giroux, 28 pages, 1992

Your toddler will be able to relate to baby and Carl, the huggable Rotweiller dog and the puppy. Mother leaves baby and puppy in the park in the care of big Carl. While Mom and her friend enjoy a cup of tea, Carl takes puppy and baby for a ride through the park. The illustrations evoke the happy era of a Renoir painting. (This is the book used in the demonstration of mother reading to her baby earlier in this chapter.)

PARENTESE TIPS AND TALKING POINTS ABOUT THE ILLUSTRATIONS:

- There is text only on the first and last pages, so you and your baby can let the detail-filled illustrations in the middle of the book inspire lots of discussion. Parents will make up the story and talk about the features you think your child will be interested in, like the merry-go-round, or the dog getting squirted by the hose. There are endless opportunities for vocabulary building and talking about experiences your child has had.

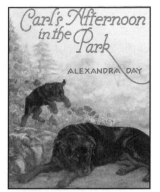

Book cover: *Carl's Afternoon in the Park*

- Since the story is wordless, you can change it each time you read it, and add more details and unusual vocabulary as your child gets older and attention increases.

- You can ask lots of questions about the visual details, like the mother in the Read-Aloud Demonstration in this chapter. If your baby responds with a babble sound, assume that your baby is talking to you and answering your question. Acknowledge what your baby says the way the mother does in the Demonstration with positive encouragement.

S
T
A
G
E
4

Animal Sounds for Baby
Cheryl Willis Hudson, illustrated by George Ford
Board book
Scholastic, 10 pages, 1995

Animal Sounds for Baby provides several features suitable for your Stage 4 Babbler. A simple three- or four-line rhyme ends in the sound the animal makes. On repeated readings your baby will be able to produce some of the animal sounds. If your child has the opportunity to visit a small petting zoo, this book will be perfect for reading before and after the visit.

PARENTESE TIPS AND TALKING POINTS ABOUT THE ILLUSTRATIONS:

- Parents can read the first three lines and wait to see if baby is ready to attempt the animal sounds.

- Reading this book in your most dramatic parentese voice will ensure that your child will enjoy the rhymes.

Mi libro pequeño de palabras
My Little Word Book
Large board book
PriddyBooks, 28 pages, 2005

This illustrated bilingual word book lends itself to any language, not only English and Spanish. There are vocabulary themes, such as action words, body words, clothes, animals, toys, food, and plants. In the back of the book is a Pronunciation Guide for Spanish words. *My Little Word Book* is a large, rather heavy board book. Parents will have to hold it or place it on the floor or table. It's too heavy for even a two-year-old to hold, but it's durable and will withstand a lot of use.

PARENTESE TIPS AND TALKING POINTS ABOUT THE ILLUSTRATIONS:

- After repeated exposures to the labels and colorful, life-like pictures, your baby will enjoy a game of "Where is?" when you ask, "Where is the camel?" Before your child can even name the pictures, she'll be able to answer your question by pointing. This is one way to learn how many words your baby understands, but cannot yet say. You'll be amazed at the amount of vocabulary in your child's little, but expanding brain.

- After your baby has a sizable English vocabulary, select a few common objects to learn in Spanish or any other language that you know. You will be amazed how fast your baby can learn a few words in another language!

STAGE 4

CHAPTER 7

Stage 5: The Word Maker

Reading to Your Communicative Twelve- to Eighteen-Month-Old

Parents will be delighted and amazed at the escalating rate of language production and understanding of their little Word Makers by around their first birthday. Of the fifty or more words that your toddler can now say, many will be those that you have read repeatedly in his favorite read-aloud books. Even if your child can't repeat every word heard of a favorite passage, he will be able to imitate the correct intonation.

In only one year, infants grow from completely dependent absorbers of their environment to mobile, demanding toddlers who can verbally communicate some of their basic needs. He'll now choose his own books from his book bin or shelf, and bring them to you to read. Then he'll let you know if he wants you to read the book again. And again. And again. He'll also let you know if he wants to hear you read the entire book or just one page, and then pick another book.

How Will Reading Aloud Be Different After Baby's First Birthday?

As you have seen in the "Read-Aloud Demonstration" in Chapter 6, the one-year-old, Olivia, is totally engaged in a dialogue with her mother, even though she cannot yet say words. She is communicating with babbling sounds, and she understands Mom's words. Olivia points to the illustrations she wants Mom to talk about. Olivia believes she is talking, and knows what she wants to say, but just can't yet verbalize the words. This is the last step just before the actual speaking of words. Mom understands what Olivia means and responds appropriately. Any moment now those babbles will turn into words.

Photo by Linda Posnick.

Read-alouds will now take on a new dimension, where more complicated vocabulary can be used as well as a longer story line or more information that your toddler can now follow. Reading before the age of one is an exercise in the rhythm and rhyme of language while helping your baby learn how to hold his attention using your voice and the illustrations. Reading after the age of one involves more teaching of vocabulary and concepts while dealing with the challenges of a more active, curious toddler.

How One Baby Shows Early Signs of Language Development (at Sixteen Months)

Sixteen-month-old Sadie loved to mimic different adult intonations. When her Mom called, "Here kitty, kitty" and then sang out, " O-l-i-v-e," Sadie would repeat the same voice, rhythm, volume, and pitch, saying the words as best she could. She knew exactly what they meant. In her high chair, when she wanted additional food, she would say "More," and then "Thank you." Some of the words she could say besides *mommy* and *daddy* were *up, down, open, moon, airplane,* and *juice.* She said *snack* when feeding a special cat treat to Olive, the kitty.

Her understanding was far greater than the words she could produce. She pointed to get Mom to do things for her. If you asked Sadie to get the mail from her toy mailbox, she walked over and got it. She shook her head "yes" or "no" in response to things she did or didn't want to do. One of her favorite books was *Where's Spot?* (See "Baby Book Reviews at a Glance" in Chapter 6.) She liked to say the word *No* under the flaps on each page.

How to Keep an Eye Out for Potential Language Difficulties

As reading teachers, we notice children in kindergarten who are experiencing difficulties hearing rhyming words, letter sounds, and names. These children might be delayed in learning how to read and might need intervention and support by specialists in speech, language, and reading. The earlier these difficulties are detected and remedied, the easier it will be for the child to progress academically. If by eighteen months your child is neither comprehending nor saying many words, you may want to consider an evaluation by a speech and language specialist. Comprehending words means that when you say familiar words your child has heard many times—such as flower, book, kitty, or teddy bear—he will respond by pointing or looking at the object. Some toddlers understand a number of words, but may not speak until later than most peers their age. Although this may be normal for your child, it's a good idea to rule out any difficulties early.

SIGNS OF POSSIBLE LANGUAGE DIFFICULTIES AT EIGHTEEN MONTHS[1]
- Avoids looking you in the eye
- Is unable to comprehend the language spoken to them
- Infrequent babbling
- Does not respond when whispered to
- Rarely imitates hand signs, such as "bye, bye"
- Little change in pitch and intensity when crying
- Is unemotional and unexpressive when saying or trying to say words

Characteristics: Twelve to Eighteen Months

Listening

- Prefers parentese to regular speech tone (see Chapter 2).
- Understands 100 to 150 words. Can say approximately fifty words, mainly nouns.
- Understands many more words than he can say. For example, if parent says *flower*, baby will turn and point to a flower but probably will not be able to say the complete word *flower* yet.
- Memory is aided by the combination of rhymes or songs with movements, such as "Itsy Bitsy Spider" and "Twinkle, Twinkle, Little Star."

- Can identify parts of the anatomy by pointing. For example, if you say, "Where is your nose?" he will point to his nose.
- Can listen with full attention when background noise is reduced and television is turned off.

Verbal

- Begins to say conventional words like *dog* instead of the sounds *(wuff wuff)*. Favorite first words might be *drink*, *eat*, *kiss*, *kitty*, *bath*, *shoe*, *dada*, and *mama*.
- Uses a variety of intonation patterns when babbling or trying to speak.
- Uses a word in different contexts. For example, will say *duck* when he sees his rubber duckie in the bathtub, a picture of a duck in a book, or a real duck in a pond.
- Uses and understands basic level words such as *dog* instead of *beagle* or *truck* instead of *cement truck*.
- Responds to your questions with pointing, body language, sounds, and some words in an attempt to have a conversation.
- Can predict some of the steps in a familiar sequence, such as getting ready for a bath or mealtime.

Photo by Linda Posnick.

Visual

- Likes to look for details in books.

Motor

- Crawls, climbs, and walks. Can crawl or walk to the bookcase and select favorite books.

Twelve-month-old is looking at the illustration of sheep behind the flap illustrating the barn door.

- Enjoys physically interacting with objects. Continues to seek out cause-and-effect situations, such as pushing a noise button or opening a flap.

- Wants to do what he sees you doing, such as sweeping the floor, giving the dog a treat, pulling the drawer handle, or getting a book and reading it.
- Enjoys moving to music.
- Points to pictures and turns pages.

Step-by-Step Read-Aloud Instructions: Twelve to Eighteen Months

Allow your toddler to select a book from a box of his favorites. You may want to include some of our recommended books from the end of this chapter.

Favorite reading positions for toddlers

- Allow your toddlers to stand, lie down, or sit while you read. At this age, some toddlers enjoy standing or leaning against a toy chest or short table where books can be placed while you read.
- Whatever position your toddler chooses, allow him to be in control and turn pages at will.
- Make it easy for your toddler to see the illustrations and interact with any textures, openings, or flaps.

Parentese interaction

- Continue reading with an expressive, deliberate voice, using sound effects for things such as animals, vehicles, and actions.
- Reread favorites such as *Good Night Gorilla*, which was introduced in Stage 4, and dramatize the elements of the sequence of the story you make up from the wordless pictures. For example, first the monkey gets the orange key (mention colors of cages and keys), then he

Photo by Linda Posnick.

Mom lying on her tummy so she can be at the same level as her seated twelve-month-old.

S
T
A
G
E
5

frees the gorilla, then the lion, and so forth. At the same time, point to the animals and name them, or ask your baby to find them, as in the example above. The black-and-white page with the different size words saying "good night" may be your child's favorite, especially if you have fun hamming it up.

• Read, chant, or sing a verse such as "Itsy Bitsy Spider" or "Twinkle, Twinkle Little Star," and teach your child the hand or body movements that accompany the verses.

• Point out familiar objects first, like animals, trucks, toys, body parts, and words that are already familiar to your baby. This will keep his attention. Then, gradually introduce new words.

Challenges

• Active toddlers enjoy pulling books out of the box, looking at them for a few seconds, and then taking more books out until the box is empty. Follow your baby's lead and build a conversation around what he is doing. Although it may not appear as if you are "reading," your baby can learn vocabulary as well as different aspects about reading, such as how to hold the book and turn pages.

Toddler enjoys pulling favorite books out of boxes and looking at the illustrations.

- If you start reading with your toddler on your lap, and he starts squirming off, that doesn't mean he wants you to stop reading. Continue reading and interacting with him as he sidles off your lap and on to the floor and crawls around. You can tell he's interested if you suddenly read in a very dramatic way and ask a question. He will probably stop what he's doing and pay attention. After you ham up the story and do all you can to make it interesting, sometimes it's best to stop reading and then try later when your toddler doesn't have his mind set on doing something else.
- Sometimes it's difficult to gain toddler's attention to begin reading. Getting a toy like a truck or animal that will be in the book will help your child become involved in the book.
- Babies become very active at this stage, and reading at bedtime, when they are tired and less active, is soothing for both baby and parent.
- Waiting in lines and in places like waiting rooms or places of worship can be difficult for toddlers as well as parents. Take books along for any occasion where you need to fill some time with an activity that is quiet and holds your child's attention. Familiar books are comforting when read in parents' arms.

Read-Aloud Demonstration: Mother Reading to Her Seventeen-Month-Old

Mom sits on floor cross-legged with her daughter, Jordan, on her lap. Jordan is very active and constantly changed positions during this reading session that lasted about ten minutes. Mother reads and interacts in an up-beat, animated way using her parentese voice by slowing her speech for emphasis, and changing volume and tone.

(Words that are read the way they appear in the book are italicized. All the other words not in italics are Mom's own words.)

We are going to read a story,
Off We Go!
    (Mom sits Jordan on her lap and begins asking questions and pointing.)
Do you see a duck? Do you see a duck?
    (Mom holds Jordan's hand and directs her hand to point to the ducks.)
Do you see two mice?

(Mom helps Jordan point and count one, two.)

Do you see a frog? I see a frog right there. Where is the frog?

(Jordan is now pointing without mother's help.)

Good job! And a bird?

(Jordan points to the bird.)

Good job!

(Jordan babbles four or five unintelligible words ending in the word "duck.")

Yes, Jordan, you see the duck. Let's open the book, *Off We Go!* Look, here is a snake and some rocks and a mouse.

(Mom points to the objects she is mentioning.)

Here is a spider. Look, Jordan, what's this?

(Jordan says, "a duck.")

Good job!

(Jordan points and says, "a cat.")

Yes, that looks like a cat but it's a mouse. Two mice. They are climbing down the grass. *Tip-toe, tippity toe, Over the leaves and down below, Off to Grandma's house we go, Sings Little Mouse.*

(Jordan babbles four or five unintelligible words ending in the word "cat.")

He kind of looks like a cat because he has whiskers, eyes, and two ears. But, he is a mouse, and he says squeak, squeak, squeak.

(Mom points to the mouse's whiskers, eyes, and ears as she talks to Jordan. Jordan becomes wiggly so Mom lies on her tummy and places Jordan close by where she can reach and point to the illustrations.)

(Jordan babbles four or five unintelligible words ending in the word "cat.")

Yes, he sort of looks like a cat.

Hip-hop, hippity hop, Through the slime and over the slop, Off to Grandma's, never stop, Sings Little Frog.

That's a frog. Do you see what this is?

(Jordan says, "bee.")

It looks like a bee. It's a fly. That's what frogs eat, flies.

(Jordan says, "bee.")

It looks like a bee because it's little, and it has wings. But it's a fly, and that is what frogs eat. They are going after those flies. Wow, look at this long tongue!

(Jordan begins to make buzzing noises and moves her hand back and forth in a flying motion.)

Is that what a fly does?

(Jordan then swats the book as she babbles several words.)

Good job! Jordan, are you swatting the fly? Show me the fly.

(Jordan points and says, "bee.")

That looks like a bee, but it's a fly.

Jordan, look, a mole!

(Jordan looks at the mole, then at Mom, and laughs.)

You think he is funny?

(Both Mom and Jordan laugh out loud.)

Mom reads three pages; then Jordan begins to turn pages. Mom follows her lead. When Jordan says "duck," Mom says, "Do you want to read the page about the duck? Let's find it." They continue skipping through the pages in which Jordan is interested, but they don't finish the book.

S
T
A
G
E
5

What to Notice in the Read-Aloud Demonstration

Notice how the mother:

- Creates most of the language above, and how relatively few of the words come straight from the book.

- Engages in conversation throughout the book, acknowledging and repeating what Jordan says, which is part babble and part understandable words like "duck" and "bee." Mother also asks questions and asks Jordan to point to some of the animals in the book.

- Gets Jordan involved in the book by holding her hand and gliding it across the page, pointing at the duck and the mice.

- Doesn't start reading the text right away, but gets Jordan involved in the book by helping her point to a familiar animal, the duck.

- Adjusts the text to the toddler's movements and present abilities. She speaks in parentese by using an excited, animated voice that sometimes pauses, slows down, or increases in volume to capture Jordan's attention.

- Helps Jordan distinguish between a bee and a fly by pointing out that the insect Jordan calls a bee is actually a fly. In this way Mom expands vocabulary by discussing bee, fly, cat, and mouse.

- Does not read the pages in order or finish the book.

- Reads a book appropriate for this stage. The book mother selected has alliteration, rhyme, rhythm, and detailed illustrations that include creatures that Jordan recognizes and can name. See "Baby Book Reviews at a Glance" below for more ideas on what to talk about when reading this book.[2]

Characteristics of Stage 5 Books

Whether rapid or gradual, each new word your toddler speaks around this age is a joy to behold. This is the stage of gradual, but increasing verbal production. In this stage, each child develops differently in terms of the number of words spoken. Every book you or your toddler selects will become an opportunity for discussion and a source of new words to learn. The types of books echo your baby's language development. For example, *Bus Stops* invites your baby to point to an object you have asked her to find. *Go Dog Go!* encourages conversation and discussion and will be useful through kindergarten or first grade as a first reader.

Your dialogue inspired by books will become more complex as your baby's language grows. Books at this stage reflect your child's interests, and will increasingly include information and concepts about the world around him. Your child may now be able to hold his attention through longer readings and follow a story from beginning to end. Books with common rhymes and songs that invite more participation, such as "Twinkle, Twinkle, Little Star," anticipate your toddler's upcoming preschool experiences.

Recommended Types of Books: Twelve to Eighteen Months

- Rhyme and song books that can be accompanied by hand movements, like "Twinkle, Twinkle, Little Star" or "I'm a Little Teapot"
- Homemade books about routines using photos, drawings, or cut-outs from catalogues or magazines
- Books that reflect your baby's experiences, such as making a peanut butter sandwich, flying a kite, or putting on rain or snow gear
- Books that label objects, toys, and parts of the body
- Books reflecting you baby's current interests
- Books in different shapes, textures, and sizes, with mirrors or noise buttons
- Books illustrating action words, such as children running, jumping, or sliding
- Books exploring space and time concepts, such as inside, under, after, and next
- Books that ask questions
- Books with one or two lines of rhythmic language on each page
- Books with common phrases such as "good-bye" and "thank you"
- Books with simple narrative structure, strong characters, events, and resolutions

S
T
A
G
E

5

Baby Book Reviews at a Glance

Caillou Tell Me Where
Fabian Savary
Board book
Chouette, 10 pages, 2000
Available in French

Book cover: *Caillou Tell Me Where*

There are several series of Caillou books, and some of them are translated into Spanish and French. This Peek-a-Boo flap series that includes Tell *Me What, Tell Me Which,* and *One or Many* is appropriate for this stage because of the questions asked in each book. In this book children hear "on" and "under" repeatedly as they search for Caillou in different parts of the house. Caillou cartoons appear on PBS.

PARENTESE TIPS AND TALKING POINTS ABOUT THE ILLUSTRATIONS:

- After you read the questions with your parentese voice, your child might point to where Caillou is hiding. After he turns the flap, read the answer on the back of the flap. The answer is a full sentence and emphasizes the word "on" or "under." To emphasize a word, read it a little bit louder, and pause after you say it to attract your child's attention to the word. Even if your child is not at the stage where he can verbalize the answers, you are providing a good model of how to answer questions. Soon he will be answering in the same way.

- This book is also available in French and Spanish. You can use the activity above to teach your baby a second language. See Chapter 9 for questions and answers about raising a bilingual child.

Where's My Sneaker?
Mercer Mayer
Board book
Random House, 19 pages, 1996

Mayer has a whole series of little critter books that have been translated into Spanish and French. In this book, Mayer's lovable Little Critter can't find his old smelly "lucky sneaker." *Where's My Sneaker?* sends us looking in the toy chest, under the bed, in the closet, and even in little sister's bubble bath. The fun is opening the flaps of the toy chest cover, the blanket, the door, and so on. Maycr's signature, whimsical, big-eyed creatures are sure to delight your baby. Unfortunately for Little Critter's Mom, he finds his sneaker where Mom wished it had stayed, in the trash can.

PARENTESE TIPS AND TALKING POINTS ABOUT THE ILLUSTRATIONS:

- This interactive flap book has an element of surprise in that the flaps are not in the same position on every page. So your toddler will be excited about looking for where the flap is on each page. There is also a different animal answering "no" under each flap. As you open the flap, parent names the animal hiding under flap, and points and reads the word, "No." Shake your head when you read, "No." Soon your baby will be shaking his head no, when you open the flap, and later on he will say, "No." The next thing he'll say is "No" as well as the animal name under the flap.

- There are little loveable details throughout the book, like the grasshopper, spider, and mouse that inspire conversations and questions. Use these details to play "Where is the _____ game?" Your child will point to what you are asking him to find. You can respond to his pointing by saying, "Yes, there's the mouse, and look, he's eating chocolate chip cookies."

Off We Go!
Jane Yolen, illustrated by Laurel Molk
Hardcover
Little, Brown and Company, 24 pages, 2000

Jane Yolen is an award-winning writer of many books for children and young adults. Full of rhythm and rhyme, *Off We Go!* offers language and illustrations your toddler will love. This book is filled with alliterations (the repetition of the beginning sounds in a number of words in a rhyme or phrase). To do the alliterative words justice, you will have to dramatize, speak clearly, and maybe use your fingers to make scratching motions, particularly in the "scritch-scratch, scritchity scratch" verses.

PARENTESE TIPS AND TALKING POINTS ABOUT THE ILLUSTRATIONS:

Book cover: *Off We Go!*

- How you read the rhymes depends on how your toddler responds. He may be so enthralled by the unusual sounds that he will be attentive through the whole book.

- An illustration may peak your toddler's interest, and he may interrupt your reading with a question. If so, stop and allow the discussion to go wherever your child takes you. He'll let you know when he wants to continue with the rest of the story.

- For the first line of alliteration of each four-line stanza, use your fingers to mimic what the animal is doing like "scritch-scratch, scritchity scratch." Scratch with the tip of your fingers on the book.

- For the third line, when it begins, "Off to grandma's house . . . " slap your hands together as you slide your top hand forward. Or think of your own movement to describe this phrase.

- Change your voice every time you read about a different animal.

More More More, Said the Baby
Vera B. Williams
Board book
Tupelo Books, 30 pages, 1990

Little Guy, Little Pumpkin, and Little Bird are whooshed up in the air and cuddled and loved by a father, grandmother, and mother. In three little stories, a baby is kissed on its belly button, held nose-to-nose in the air, or rocked back and forth. Each time the baby says, "More. More. More." The colorful illustrations, done in gouache paintings with hand-painted lettering, convey the warmth of emotions we express to our babies.

PARENTESE TIPS AND TALKING POINTS ABOUT THE ILLUSTRATIONS:

- When reading to your twelve- to eighteen-month-old toddler, ask him if he wants to fly or swing like the toddler in the story. Being chased is a fun game at this age, and in the book the toddlers start to run away, and then are caught, lifted up, swung around, and hugged just like in real life.

- The rhyme can also be sung like a rap. While you're engaged in a chasing game, take the opportunity to verbalize everything you're doing, and use words like "up," "down," "run," "stop," "go," and so on.

Peanut Butter and Jelly
Traditional song illustrated by Robin Oz
Paperback
Puffin Books, 23 pages, 1992

After you have read this book a number of times, your toddler may be able to imitate some of the luscious words under the active, busy illustrations: *squash them, mash them,* and so on. Hopefully most parents will know the tune, because this particular book does not include the music. However, you don't need to sing. You can get just as dramatic an effect by saying the lines as if they were part of a poem.

PARENTESE TIPS AND TALKING POINTS ABOUT THE ILLUSTRATIONS:

- When you make your toddler a sandwich, you can sing or chant *Peanut Butter*. If you are not making the real thing, create hand movements to depict *knead, spread, slice,* and *eat*. The whole point of this book is that it is teaching toddlers descriptive vocabulary through an everyday activity.

- This book is very interactive because toddlers can be involved by pretending to make not only peanut butter sandwiches, but any kind of sandwich. You are teaching new vocabulary as you add different ingredients to your make-believe silly sandwiches. For example, use your hands as slices of bread, and pick up anything around, and say, "Let's make a shoe sandwich," or a "book sandwich."

- When you actually make real peanut butter or other sandwiches, you can sing the "Peanut Butter Song" to recall the book. Make up new words depending on the real-life ingredients. Read the book together after lunch.

S
T
A
G
E
5

Go, Dog. Go!
P.D. Eastman
Hardcover
Random House, 64 pages, 1961
Available in Spanish

In the style of a Dr. Seuss book, with a vocabulary simplified for a beginning reader, *Go, Dog. Go!* is fun for a one-and-a-half-year-old toddler because of its short, terse sentences and eye-catching, simple drawings. The humorous drawings belie the simple text. There is plenty in the colorful drawings to talk and laugh about. This book is also available in Spanish. If you can read Spanish, once your toddler is familiar with the English version, you can read the Spanish version. You will be amazed at how fast your toddler will learn some words in Spanish.

PARENTESE TIPS AND TALKING POINTS ABOUT THE ILLUSTRATIONS:

- Many questions can be asked: How many dogs? What color is that dog? Is that one big or little?

- Let your toddler finish the fun sentences: "Three dogs down in the _____ (water)." Your toddler can grow with this book until he can read it independently.

- Your toddler can practice saying "hello" and "good-bye" as well as concept words such as over, under, around, fast, and slow.

Twinkle, Twinkle, Little Star
Told and illustrated by Iza Trapani
Board book, Paperback
Whispering Coyote Press, 26 pages, 1994
Available in Spanish

Wonder and mystery are the qualities that stimulate our imagination and cause us to want to know and to explore. How many great thinkers through the ages have looked at a star with a sense of wonder? This simple, old, yet cosmic rhyme has become a chanting ritual to generations of babies and toddlers.

Book cover: *Twinkle, Twinkle, Little Star*

PARENTESE TIPS AND TALKING POINTS ABOUT THE ILLUSTRATIONS:

- In addition to the simple basic rhyme we all know, this book provides new stanzas, all illustrated in a way that will stimulate conversation about stars, planets, and the night. Talk about the moon, which is something babies can point to early on. You can also talk about the night and that most creatures sleep at night, but some, like owls and coyotes, stay awake.

- As you sing "twinkle, twinkle," open and shut both hands to imitate a twinkling star. Relate to real life experiences by going out at night, looking at the stars, and notice the twinkling, as you sing the rhyme in the book.

- The musical notation is printed on the last page for those who are unfamiliar with the tune. If you can play an instrument, such as a guitar or piano, as you sing, your baby or toddler will be transfixed by both the words and music.

Jamberry
Bruce Degen
Board book
Harper Festival, 26 pages, 1995

A newborn can delight in the sounds of berry rhymes as well as a toddler. Adults as well as toddlers will enjoy the illustrations full of fun and action by author-illustrator Bruce Degan. In an endnote, the author tells us how he was inspired by picking berries in the fields and bringing them home to make berry pies and jams.

PARENTESE TIPS AND TALKING POINTS ABOUT THE ILLUSTRATIONS:

- What's important about this book is the beautiful rhythm and rhyme of each page, which demands to be read at a steady, natural pace and tone. The more you read it, and the more your toddler hears it, the more you'll both like it. The nonsensical, but harmonious, rhymes grow on you. The nonsensical feature will capture your toddler's attention, because it's like nothing they have heard before.

- The illustrations are equally nonsensical, and stimulate descriptive conversation. There's a blueberry waterfall, bread growing on trees, and waffle lily pads. The book will have new meaning if toddlers can taste some blueberries, strawberries, raspberries, or blackberries. Better yet, if they can pick them, they'll have an even broader experience.

- Another word game you can play is to add the word berry to anything you see, like "trainberry" and "trackberry." For example, you can say, "milkberry, duckberry, daddyberry, or anythingberry."

Tumble Bumble
Felicia Bond
Board book
Harper Festival, 30 pages, 1996

At a stage when your baby is becoming a toddler and absorbing many new words every day, he will insist that you read *Tumble Bumble* repeatedly. With such words as strolled, grinned, introduced, apologized, and startled, your toddler is gaining vocabulary in a way only books read repeatedly can offer. Soon your toddler will memorize the rhymes and read along with you "They all began to dance a jig and bumped into a baby pig." The clear, joyous illustrations are filled with details toddlers love to point to and talk about: the animals and the half-eaten food items in a messy kitchen.

PARENTESE TIPS AND TALKING POINTS ABOUT THE ILLUSTRATIONS:

- To do the rhyme justice, read each stanza until you finish, and then you can stop and talk. There is a flow that is best followed in order to get the rhyme and the meaning.

- When you read passages that contain a word or two that you think your toddler may not understand, don't feel you have to stop and explain every word. Toddlers will get the gist of your words by your intonation and emphasis, and by looking at the pictures. Children who listen to repeated readings of rich book language have an advantage, because they eventually absorb it.

Hand Rhymes
Marc Brown
Board book
Puffin Unicorn Books, 31 pages, 1985

Babies and toddlers enjoy songs and rhymes with finger play. Marc Brown collected and illustrated fourteen rhymes with accompanying instructive icons (little pictures to show you what to do with your hands) next to the lines of verse. There is a rhyme for each season, including "Jack-O-Lantern" and "Little Goblins," as well as several about babies. There is a companion to this book by the same author-illustrator, *Finger Rhymes*.

PARENTESE TIPS AND TALKING POINTS ABOUT THE ILLUSTRATIONS:

- Look at the little icons to see what motion your hands and fingers should make. The more you say the rhyme and perform the hand motions, the more comfortable you'll be. You'll also know which rhymes your toddler likes best. Subtle voice effects like volume changes or different facial expressions will also add to the hand motions.

- Feel free to use only one of the hand motions, instead of all. Pick one that seems to capture the essence of the whole rhyme and use that if it seems more comfortable for you.

¿Quién se esconde?
Emanuela Bussolati
Board book
Editorial Edaf Antillas, S.A., 22 pages, 2002

This unusually designed board book is constructed so the right side of book is fanned out and rounded, allowing your toddler to easily open one of the rainbow-colored pages. Each page asks "Quién se esconde?" (Who is hiding?). Behind each of the flaps is the answer along with the illustration. Each page gives a simple illustration, without background distractions. Although this is a pattern book, each page offers several interesting vocabulary words for your toddler to learn in Spanish. This ¡Abre las ventanas! Flap book series includes three other titles that also ask questions.

S
T
A
G
E
5

PARENTESE TIPS AND TALKING POINTS ABOUT THE ILLUSTRATIONS:

- Once you've read this book several times, and your child is familiar with the vocabulary, read the text, leaving out one of the words.
  For example, ¿Quién se esconde entre las ramas de la encina? Una _____ (ardilla).
  Who is hiding in the oak tree? A _____ (squirrel).

- You could play the same game leaving out the different words.
  For example, ¿Quién se esconde entre las ramas de la _____ (encina)?
  Who is hiding in the _____ (oak tree)?

- Though not a bilingual book (available only in Spanish), you could make questions in any language, and provide your own answers, creating as rich a vocabulary as you think your toddler is ready to learn.

- If you're making up your own words, be sure to include words like under, behind, between, and so on.

S
T
A
G
E
5

CHAPTER 8

Stage 6: The Phrase Maker

Reading to Your Verbal Eighteen- to Twenty-Four-Month-Old

Your family's involvement with books is showing results. Your toddler loves books and has identified her favorites. Her speaking language reflects some of the words from books that have been read repeatedly. Your toddler can now say or point to the names of many zoo and farm animals, foods, toys, various components of trucks and construction vehicles, and everyday objects in her life. Family conversation often revolves around what was learned or read in books. Although the amount of words spoken at this time varies, you can rest assured that your toddler understands most of your conversations and the language of books that have been read to her.

Family conversations that revolve around your child's interests demonstrate that you acknowledge the importance or your children's contribution to family activities

Photo by Linda Posnick.

and talk. It's important, therefore, that parents encourage talk through questioning. Research indicates that parents who promote conversation and dialogue through questions raise children who talk more and talk earlier.[1] Books provide a readily available forum for questions and conversation.

At this stage you'll notice your toddler's attention span increasing. You'll be reading many more books more often during the day. By the time your toddler reaches two, you will have read hundreds of books with incalculable numbers of words. This adds up to untold numbers of brain connections that create good language and problem-solving skills. Part of these skills involve knowing the proper syntax (word order) of their language. These are skills that are crucial to future reading and writing abilities.

How to Encourage Your Toddler's Life Experiences Around Books

When nineteen-month-old Fernando had an interest in trains, the family embarked on an intense study of trains through books, museums, and train rides. Trucks absorbed twenty-three month-old Gavin. His parents acquired every truck and construction vehicle book published, and Gavin could name and point to the various types of trucks and their parts. This interest resulted in field trips to construction sites and automobile museums. Two-year-old Melissa loved cats. Her parents took her to the zoo to see the lions and tigers and taught Melissa about other members of the cat family.

This toddler is obsessed with trucks. Having heard this truck book read to him repeatedly, he memorized the words and can now "read" it independently.

Based on their toddler's interest, some parents use the themes of books to design their children's birthday parties. For example, for her son's second birthday, one parent read *The Three Billy Goats Gruff* and created a scavenger hunt based on the characters and setting in the book. The party was held in a park that had a creek with a bridge over it. Older children followed the clues to the prizes, and the younger children and parents followed. The treasure and party favors included a book for each child.

How to Respond When Your Child Mispronounces a Word

Now that your little Phrase Maker is beginning to put words together that have been stored away in her brain over the past two years, you may be wondering about some of the mispronunciations you're hearing. You may be comparing your child with other children her age. The following chart gives you a time framework for ages in which various sounds can be produced. Every child is unique and will learn the correct sounds according to her own inner time clock. You'll notice that r's and l's usually are not pronounced correctly until six years of age.

If your child pronounces a sound in a word incorrectly, just repeat what your child said, but say the sounds correctly. For example, if your child says "twuck" for truck or "yion" for lion, you say a sentence with the words correctly pronounced in the natural course of your conversation and let it go at that. Please note that the "r" and the "l" are difficult to enunciate sounds, and will eventually be pronounced correctly by six years of age. Your child is gradually trying to get her mouth to pronounce words the way she hears them. In other words, don't make a big deal out of it. Your job is to be a model of good language and correct pronunciation.

Ages When Sounds Are Produced[2]

Sounds produced during the first 2 years
p   m   h   n   w   b

Sounds that may not sound adult-like until between ages 3 and 6
r   l

Sounds that don't emerge until between ages 2 and 4
k   g   d   t

Sounds that appear between 2.5 and 4 years
f   y

Sounds that appear between 3.5 and 8 years
ch   sh   z   j   v

S
T
A
G
E

Characteristics: Eighteen to Twenty-Four Months

Listening

- Prefers parentese to regular speech tone (see Chapter 2).
- Understands about 200 words and continues to learn meanings of several new words every day.
- Still loves to hear her favorite rhymes and songs repeated.
- Can listen with full attention when background noise is reduced and television is turned off.

Verbal

- Can say an average of 50 to 170 words.
- There is a surge of mental development at this age that results in the ability to think, reason, and speak words more clearly.
- Imitates expressions such as "Uh, oh!"
- Learns to say about sixty-three new words a week after learning first fifty words.
- Learns the structure of language, such as how to form a question and the proper word order of a sentence. However, may not yet be able to express this language.
- Uses words for common objects: foods, animals, body anatomy, clothing, and toys. Starts using action words such as *run, dance,* and *see,* modifiers such as *hot* and *more,* and social words such as *thank you* and *no.*
- Begins to ask "What's that?" Knows that objects have names. Can name family members.
- Begins to combine nouns and verbs to make two-word phrases or sentences.
- Learns new words through conversations about daily experiences and from hearing books read aloud.
- Is strongly dependent on body language to communicate while she is acquiring verbal language.
- Still can't pronounce correctly some of the longer words she knows, like *helicopter.* She may say the right number of syllables but may not be able to pronounce some of the letter sounds yet.
- Emulates whatever you say with excitement (even swear words!).
- Girls often understand and produce more words earlier than boys. They may also produce longer and more complex sentences. Boys will soon catch up.

- Begins using more specific names, like *pickup truck* and *SUV* instead of saying the category name *car*.
- Responds verbally to your naming and labeling of objects when visiting various locations, such as the park, the zoo, friends' homes, grocery shopping, etc.

Visual

- Is captivated by the intricate, detailed illustrations in books like those of Richard Scarry.

Motor

- Imitates what you do around the house, such as cleaning the table with a paper towel, vacuuming the carpet, mowing the lawn, or reading a book or newspaper.
- There is also an increase in physical ability: toddler runs faster, turns knobs, and turns pages in a book one at a time.

Step-by-Step Read-Aloud Instructions: Eighteen to Twenty-four Months

Allow your toddler to select a book from a box of her favorites. You may want to include some of our recommended books from the end of this chapter.

Favorite reading positions for toddlers

- Follow your toddler's lead by allowing her to stand, lie down, or sit while you read aloud. Whatever position she chooses, allow your toddler to be in control and turn pages at will.

Parentese

- Continue reading with an expressive voice, using your best attempts at verbal sound effects for animals, vehicles, and actions.
- Model correct pronunciation of favorite words, like *helicopter,* very distinctly: "hel-i-cop-ter." She will need to hear some words many times before she can say them correctly.
- Read your child's favorites, such as truck, train, or animal books. Repeated readings help toddlers learn specialized vocabulary. Instead of the categorical name *truck*, they learn more specific names, like *excavator* and *bulldozer*.

- Read, chant, or sing familiar and new rhymes with hand and body movements. Some of the sing-along rhymes that are learned in nursery school can be practiced at home.
- Slide your finger under words on the page to show your toddler left to right movement so that she can learn that the black marks on the page have meaning. Use picture books as a source of new words that you make up as you interpret the illustrations.

Challenges

- Toddlers enjoy pulling books out of the box or shelf, looking at them for a few seconds, and then taking more books out until the books are all over the floor. Follow your baby's lead and build conversation around his activity. Although it may not appear as if you are "reading," your baby can learn vocabulary as well as different aspects about reading, such as how to hold the book correctly and turn pages.
- If your child can't decide which book she wants to hear, and keeps switching from one book to another while you read, go ahead and switch to another book. Follow what your child wants to hear and look at. Your job is to keep interacting with conversation, giving your child attention and loving understanding. This is how you build a love of books and all the words that go with it.
- There is a wide range in attention span at this age. Some children can listen attentively for a half hour, and others can only listen for thirty seconds. Also your toddler's attention span will vary from day to day. Be patient and understanding. Most of the time, hearing a familiar story is calming, and you'll notice that if your child is having a difficult few moments, the sound of your reading voice will calm her down.
- Waiting in lines and in places like waiting rooms and places of worship can be difficult for toddlers as well as parents. Take books along for any occasion where you need to fill some time with an activity that is quiet and holds your child's attention. Familiar books are comforting when read in parents' arms.

Read-Aloud Demonstration: Father Reading to His Two-Year-Old

In our parent workshops, we noticed a number of parents of two- and three-year-olds who merely read books straight through without responding to their toddler's verbal or nonverbal reactions to the book. Unless parents interact with their toddlers, it's easy for the child to lose interest. By restating what the child said, the parent below acknowledged his child making a connection that rockets go to the moon. It's important that parents know it's okay for their child to make the book fun by getting up and jumping around.

(Words that are read the way they appear in the book are italicized. All the other words not in italics are dad's own words.)

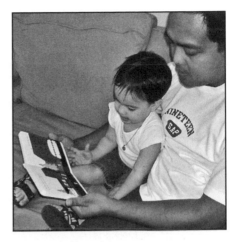

Look! There's a little car in this book like your car. Come see!
> (Toddler sits down on couch next to dad. He looks and points at illustration of car and makes a vroom, vroom sound.)
> (Dad skips around through the pages of the book until he finds some objects that he knows Dylan will be interested in.)

Look, there's a helicopter. Can you find it? Do you think it's landing or taking off?
> (Dad makes motions with his hand going up and down.)
> (Toddler imitates dad's movements making babbling sounds, trying to say helicopter by saying, "hejja up up.")

Yes, helicopters go up and fly around in the sky.

Look what's on this page. Can you find the rocket? Five, four, three, two, one, blast off!
> (Dad makes a rocket with his fist, and makes a swishing sound for a rocket taking off.)
> (Child follows dad's finger and babbles several words ending in the "up moon.")

Yes, Dylan, rockets go up in space to the moon. Let's find the cover of the book. Where do you think the bus is going? Let's open the book and see.

The bus stops at the beach. An artist steps off. Can you find two sailboats?
> (Dad points to the sailboats and counts. Then Dylan puts his finger on the sailboats. Dad and Dylan point together and dad counts, "one, two.")

(Dylan says, "boat" and counts "one, two." Dylan turns a couple pages to the construction site.)

Wow! Cranes lifting heavy beams.

(Dad points and says, "Look, Dylan, cranes like the one we saw today on the freeway.")

(Dylan looks intently and points and says, "big crane.")

The bus stops at a building site. Four construction workers leap off.

(Dad makes leaping motions with his hand while counting one, two, three, four construction workers.)

(Dylan laughs as father does leaping motions with his hand.)

(Dylan says, "jump, jump" and gets up to show dad how he can jump.)

Can you find a bulldozer?

There's a tiny, tiny bulldozer, Dylan. Can you find the orange bulldozer?

(Dylan looks over every bit of the page, and bursts with excitement when he finds the bulldozer, babbling something that tries to express bulldozer over and over.)

The same type of interaction continues throughout the book as Dylan looks, points, and babbles responses to the book's questions. He continues to get excited as he discovers new vehicles, like a pickup truck with a cow and an ambulance. He also points to the animals in the illustrations and makes animal noises. After finishing the book, dad asked Dylan to go back through the book and point to and name the places where the bus had stopped. If Dylan didn't know the name of a place, dad would name it and Dylan repeated.[3]

What to Notice in the Read-Aloud Demonstration

Notice how the father:

- Engages this very active toddler by asking him to come see a car in the book that is like his toy car.
- Interjects his own words, sounds, and movements related to the illustrations in this book.
- Adjusts the text to the toddler. He also speaks in parentese by using an excited, animated voice that sometimes pauses, slows down, or increases in volume to capture Dylan's attention.
- Acknowledges how Dylan knew that rockets could go to the moon by verifying what Dylan said.

- Engages in conversation throughout the book, constantly questioning Dylan and pulling him into the conversation.
- Helps Dylan learn the names of the places where the bus stops by reviewing the book again after the first reading.
- Teaches concepts such as numbers.
- Skips pages until he finds one he knows will interest Dylan.
- Selects a book based on Dylan's specific interests such as vehicles, construction sites, and rockets.

See "Baby Book Reviews at a Glance" below for more ideas on what to talk about when reading this book and others.

Characteristics of Stage 6 Books

The books your toddler enjoys at this stage are many and varied. She may still want to hear rhymes or board books she heard at birth, while at the same time showing an interest in adult books with pictures and illustrations you can talk about. At this stage your toddler will likely surprise you with the wide range of books she is attracted to.

Now your toddler can sit through and attend to books with longer stories, more complicated language with alliterative sounds. Books that feature concepts that are generally taught in preschool, such as numbers from one to ten and colors, are good for this stage. Your toddler will also be interested in books that include specialized vocabulary, such as cooking ingredients, truck and train parts, body anatomy, and insect, bird, or plant names. The worlds of imagination, humor, objects, living creatures, and concepts are opening up to your child in a way they never could without access to the books you've read aloud over the past two years.

At every stage of their development, children exhibit a variety of differences. Some children at this stage can give their attention comfortably for long periods and ask you to read the same book again and again, while others can barely focus attention through a short book. Toddlers who have been read to since birth are more likely to be accustomed to reading as part of their everyday world and routine. If you read with a voice full of joy and fun and find the right book—one that will hold your child's attention, regardless of how easily distracted she usually is—she will be drawn in by its magic. That book may be the one that encourages your toddler down the yellow brick road to the enchanted world of books.

Recommended Types of Books: Eighteen to Twenty-Four Months

- Books with complex pictures that you can talk about, like Richard Scarry books or young adult or adult books that show cross-sections of ships or airplanes (*National Geographic,* travel books, or your local zoo publications).
- Books about your toddler's current interests, such as trucks, trains, animals, babies, and favorite characters.
- Books illustrating action words such as running, jumping, or sliding.
- Rhyme and song books that can be accompanied by hand or body movements, like *Itsy Bitsy Spider* and *I'm a Little Tea Pot.*
- Books showing children doing common chores around the house or that open the door to talking about toddler's own experiences at home (even misbehaving).
- Books showing various feelings (happy, sad, angry, jealous) either through the story or through illustrations that you can discuss with your toddler.
- Poetic books with tantalizing language written by well-known children's book authors.
- Books exploring space and time concepts, such as inside, under, after, and next.
- Number, color, and vocabulary concept books.
- Longer stories with more complicated rhymes and alliteration.
- Books with interesting language that is just a little beyond the toddler's conversational language.

Baby Book Reviews at a Glance

No, David!
David Shannon
Hardcover
Blue Sky Press, 30 pages, 1998
Available in Spanish

It seems children of all ages (including adults) love *No, David!* They can relate to an innocent, but out-of-control, toddler, whose mother implores him to "settle down." First and second graders as well as one-and-a-half- or three-year-olds want to look at *No, David!* again and again. Your toddler may have the simple fifty-four-word text memorized after one or two readings. Perhaps your child will have internalized this book, so that when she is transgressing she'll yell out "No, David!" and everyone, including Mom, will laugh. David Shannon's illustrations are, in a word, hilarious. In an author's note, David Shannon reveals that *No, David!* is autobiographical. Indeed, it could be the biography of many of our toddlers at least once in their lives.

PARENTESE TIPS AND TALKING POINTS ABOUT THE ILLUSTRATIONS:

- Read the voice of Mom with authority and expression.

- Your toddler will stop on every page and want to talk about the muddy tracks on the carpeting, the overflowing bathtub, and especially David running down the street with no clothes on.

- Every page is full of illustrations of behaviors that might help your child understand why parents sometimes get upset.

- Talk about consequences for what David is doing, and your own home behavioral guidelines.

- Talk about feelings such as mad, sad, happy, and content.

Mrs. Wishy-Washy
Joy Cowley, illustrated by Elizabeth Fuller
Board book
Philomel Books, 15 pages, 1999

Many kindergartners and first-graders have read *Mrs. Wishy-Washy* and ask to read it again and again. We recommend it for eighteen to twenty-four months, but try it on your younger baby and observe her reactions. The illustrations are simple and bright enough for a younger baby, and the language will hold your toddler's attention. Joy Cowley is a master of crafting just the right sounds and words to be dramatized by the reader. She has written dozens of little reading books for beginning readers that your child may encounter in kindergarten and first grade.

PARENTESE TIPS AND TALKING POINTS ABOUT THE ILLUSTRATIONS:

- As soon as she can talk, encourage your child to memorize some of the pages. You can do this by reading certain pages over several times. Almost any page lends itself to memorization.

- Mrs. Wishy-Washy wants to wash the mud off her dirty animals, but they don't cooperate. This is one book you may find that you pretty much stick to the text as is. However, you'll want to draw out the wiiiiiisshhy, waaaasshhy and make scrubbing motions with your hands.

- When you give your child a bath, say, "wishy, washy" while you are scrubbing. Then say "Away went the cow," and so on, to help your child remember the phrases.

- Your toddler can also say, "wishy, washy" when she scrubs her toys in the bath if you show her how first.

Bus Stops
Taro Gomi
Board book
Chronicle Books, 32 pages, 1988

This book was translated from Japanese. It was first published in Tokyo under the title *Basu Ga Kita* in 1985. This is a story about a bus that stops all around town. An artist "*steps* off" at the beach, a salesman "*hops* off" at the edge of town, four construction workers "*leap* off" at a building site. A different verb is used for each person who leaves the bus, thus modeling to your toddler the variety of vocabulary that can be used for the same action.

Book cover: *Bus Stops*

PARENTESE TIPS AND TALKING POINTS ABOUT THE ILLUSTRATIONS:

- What your toddler will really love about this book is the question after each person steps off the bus: "Can you find the bulldozer? Can you find the helicopter?" Your toddler will love pointing to the simple, graphic illustrations.

- On each page you read, clarify any unusual words you think your toddler might not be familiar with, for example, "the edge of town." Point to the edge of town in the picture and say the phrase differently. For example, you could say, "near the town." You might think this is kind of young to go into this kind of explanation, but you're setting a precedent for a process you'll be using from now on.

The Itsy Bitsy Spider
Iza Trapani
Board book, Paper
Whispering Coyote Press, 27 pages, 1993

In this version, *Itsy Bitsy Spider* not only climbed up the waterspout, but also up the wall, the pail, the rocking chair, the tree, and finally ended up on her web. There are several published versions of this beloved rhyme, but this one has a fun twist. Trapani's watercolors are realistic and inviting, full of sunshine and warmth. There is even a musical score at the end for parents to follow the well-known tune. Toddlers love the classic song and rhyme and the hand motions that can accompany them. This is one of the classics, along with *Twinkle, Twinkle, Little Star,* that children learn in

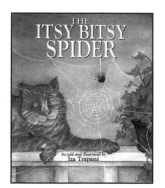

Book cover: *The Itsy Bitsy Spider*

preschool, but they can memorize the song between one-and-a-half and two-and-a-half years depending on how early your toddler begins talking in sentences.

PARENTESE TIPS AND TALKING POINTS ABOUT THE ILLUSTRATIONS:

• Use your fingers to imitate a spider climbing and then being washed out of the spout. Here's what you do: Place your pinky from one hand onto the thumb of your other hand like a spider climbing up and up. Release the pinky and thumb, twist your hand around and join the pinky and thumb again. When the rain and spider are washed out of the spout, make a wooshing, sweeping motion with your arms. Make a circular shape with your arms for the sun. And then do the climbing motion again.

• Besides the song, talk about what happens to the spider in other scenes. Your child will tell you what she wants to hear about. If she isn't talking yet, she'll point or look intently at something. That is your cue to talk about what she is looking at.

Barnyard Dance
Sandra Boynton
Board book
Workman Publishing, 20 pages, 1993

Book cover: *Barnyard Dance*

If the illustrations in this book look familiar, it is because you may have received a greeting card by Sandra Boynton. This particular Boynton book came to our attention during one of our visits to the bookstore. We saw an eighteen-month-old baby girl dancing along as her mother chanted the book. This parent and others have told us that the Boynton books are some of their toddlers' favorites.

Most babies and toddlers love music from before they were born. Once they start walking (and even before), it isn't long before they begin moving their bodies to the rhythm of the beat. *Barnyard Dance* invites you and your toddler to read and move together to the rhythm of the beat.

PARENTESE TIPS AND TALKING POINTS ABOUT THE ILLUSTRATIONS:

- Do what the animals do in the book: You and your child will bow, twirl, bounce, and strut, etc.

- Use parentese when you read the animal noises (use your funniest, exaggerated voice).

- You and your toddler will have fun chanting as you move in concert with the bouncy rhythms.

- You may find yourselves calling out this chant as you walk down the aisles of a store or anywhere you're walking together like the child and parent we saw in the bookstore.

Ten, Nine, Eight
Molly Bang
Paperback
Mulberry Books, 21 pages, 1983

Counting backwards from 10, father's gentle rhymes send a little girl to sleep. Everything about this book is peaceful, a way for your toddler to settle down to get ready for bed. Molly Bang's illustrations are rather subdued and understated, yet powerful. There is the sense of love and comfort from everything in the little girl's room. At eighteen to twenty-four months your toddler may be learning to count as well as sing the alphabet song.

PARENTESE TIPS AND TALKING POINTS ABOUT THE ILLUSTRATIONS:

- In the first illustration of the two feet with the ten toes, count each toe, and then touch and count each of your toddler's toes.

- On the next page with the nine toys including the cat, look around your child's room and find toys or other objects to count. Every page has objects like those in your child's room to count before going to bed.

The Fantastic Cutaway Book of Flight
Jon Richards
Paperback
Copper Beech Books, 40 pages, 1998

You may wonder why we included a book that a young adult or adult would read. At eighteen to twenty-four months, your toddler can be interested in more than cute, albeit wonderful, baby books. So be on the lookout for other types of books with large illustrations that you think reflect your toddler's interests. When you take your toddler to the bookstore or library, he or she may select a book with text that is too complicated, but with illustrations that are enticing. Children of this age are known to pull books on subjects such as mountain climbing or travel off the shelves and want to hear about the pictures. This is another way to learn new vocabulary words.

PARENTESE TIPS AND TALKING POINTS ABOUT THE ILLUSTRATIONS:

- If your toddler loves truck, train, or airplane books, then he will be fascinated by the cutaway illustrations of the Hindenburg dirigible, a Fokker triplane, or the B-2 stealth bomber. You look at the text to get any information you think your toddler would want to hear.

- You don't read the text as is, but "translate" it into language she can understand. Your toddler will let you know what she is interested in. Don't be surprised if she asks you to "read" this repeatedly.

- Talk to your child about size, color words, and descriptive words.

- You will be using words your toddler doesn't know, like rotor or passenger cabin. Talk about these words. Explain them so that your toddler can use them. With their advanced number of brain connections, don't be surprised how fast your toddler will learn these words after hearing them just a few times.

Diggers and Dump Trucks
Angela Royston
Hardcover
Little Simon, 16 pages, 1991

If your toddler loves trucks, she will ask you to read *Diggers and Dump Trucks* again and again through the ages of three or four. More than naming the parts (shovel, bucket, mudguard, leg), each earth-moving machine has a description of its function. A photo gives a clear side view, and a drawing shows what the excavator or truck does.

PARENTESE TIPS AND TALKING POINTS ABOUT THE ILLUSTRATIONS:

- Toddlers at this stage will take a book like this and go right to the page they are interested in. Notice what your child is interested in and either read the text or talk about what she is looking at. Or do both. Use the vocabulary in the book to ask questions during your conversations. For example, ask, "Can you find the forks in this forklift?" Your toddler will learn these labels quickly, if this is a subject she or he is interested in.

- You can point to the tiny man next to the giant dump truck and talk about the driver's size compared to the wheel, and about how the driver has to climb a ladder to get into the cab. For a toddler, this is serious business.

Down by the Station
Will Hillenbrand
Hardcover
Harcourt, 40 pages, 1999

This story, based on the traditional song *Down by the Station*, is essentially a wordless picture book. You can talk about the illustrations or you can sing or chant the lyrics. Your child may prefer a discussion about the pictures. Toddlers will love the illustrations reminiscent of those in *Curious George*, as they search for and point to the balloon and monkey throughout the story. At every station the train halts to pick up another happy creature. But tension mounts as the baby seal and penguin jump into the water inhabited by crocodiles. Just in time both are saved and eventually arrive at the children's zoo. The notes to the original song are on the last page.

Book cover: *Down by the Station*

PARENTESE TIPS AND TALKING POINTS ABOUT THE ILLUSTRATIONS:

- Talk about the animal names, train, train track, smoke, and whistle.

- Find the balloon on each page.

- What is the monkey up to on every page?

- Note the animals waving "bye, bye" as they board the train. Imitate hand movements.

- Say something like, "Uh, oh" and talk about how the penguin jumps into the crocodile-infested waters, and what is going to happen to him! Explain how the zookeeper is coming to save the baby penguin.

- Talk about children getting off the school bus—what are the boys or girls wearing or carrying?

Read-Aloud Rhymes for the Very Young
Selected by Jack Prelutsky, illustrated by Marc Brown
Hardcover
Random House, 98 pages, 1986

Poetry can easily be overlooked beyond the nursery rhyme stage. These read-aloud rhymes are full of fun, good laughs, unusual vocabulary, and all kinds of learning opportunities. The subjects range from animal habitats, weather, shadows, dragons, birthdays, holidays, and much more.

There is a poem for almost any phase of a toddler's world, imaginary or real. The poems begin with getting up in the morning and end with Good Night, Good Night. The poems were selected by poet Jack Prelutsky, and offer a wide representation of favorite poets, including Dr. Seuss, Lewis Carroll, Mary Ann Hoberman, and Robert Louis Stevenson. The illustrations by Marc Brown will serve as a magnet to get your toddler into the rhymes. Jim Trelease, the best-selling author of *The Read Aloud Handbook*, wrote the introduction.

We selected this book of rhymes for stage six because many of the poems are shorter in length. Active toddlers sometimes have short attention spans.

PARENTESE TIPS AND TALKING POINTS ABOUT THE ILLUSTRATIONS:

- Allow toddler to select the picture she wants to discuss.

- Parents can then read the rhyme that goes with the illustration.

STAGE 6

- If your toddler interrupts and wants to extend the discussion beyond the rhyme, please follow your child's lead. You never know where it will take you.

- Sometime toddlers get excited about the illustrations, and will only listen to a few lines. They will then point to another illustration, and want you to read a few lines from the next poem. It's okay not to finish the whole poem and skip around.

Five Little Monkeys Jumping on the Bed
Eileen Christelow
Board Book
Houghton Mifflin, 28 pages, 1989
Available in Spanish

Most toddlers love jumping on their beds after putting on their pajamas and getting ready for their bedtime stories. So they will love this countdown chant that begins: "Then . . . five little monkeys jumped on the bed!"

By age two, your toddler may begin to chime in as you read and echo the easily remembered lines that count backwards from five. Your child will especially love the ending when Mom, out of relief, jumps up and down on her bed. At stage six, your toddler will enjoy the humorous colored pencil drawings and will relate to the familiar routines of monkeys taking a bath, putting on their pajamas, and brushing their teeth.

PARENTESE TIPS AND TALKING POINTS ABOUT THE ILLUSTRATIONS:

- After several readings, when child and parent have become familiar with the rhyme, you may chant without the book, using exaggerated hand movements. For example, hold out your five fingers, and every time a monkey falls off the bed you hide one finger. Then you make believe you are bumping your head with your fist. You make a telephone out of your hand and fingers and put it against your ear. Then shake your fingers no, when there are no more monkeys jumping out of bed.

- Talk about feelings, crying, being happy, sad, or worried. For example, monkeys cry when they fall off the bed.

STAGE 6

Fuzzytail Friends Lift-and-Look Animal Book
Illustrated by Lisa McCue
Large board book with flaps
Random House, 10 pages, 1997

At this stage your toddler is rapidly learning new words each day. *Fuzzytail Friends* gives the opportunity to pick up new vocabulary in one of the most entertaining ways possible, lifting flaps while parent reads the label revealed underneath the flap. With over fifty flaps, there are words to learn under the categories of the farm, the garden, the forest, the shore, and the pond. The thick cardboard pages make this book indestructible and able to withstand repeated toddler manipulations.

PARENTESE TIPS AND TALKING POINTS ABOUT THE ILLUSTRATIONS:

- On the farm page, emphasize the names of baby farm animals and how it's different from the name of the adult animal. For example, piglet and pig, duckling and duck, etc.

- On the garden page, talk about counting the bugs hidden under flaps.

- On the forest page, discuss the animal homes, such as bear den, rabbit burrow, and so on.

- On the sea life page, talk about concepts dealing with opposites, such as in and out, etc. Make sentences out of words on the front and back of flaps so your child hears concepts used repeatedly.

Where Do Balloons Go? An Uplifting Mystery
Jamie Lee Curtis
Hardcover
HarperCollins, 33 pages, 2000
Available in Spanish

Where Do Balloons Go? An Uplifting Mystery is magical and full of ideas to ponder and question. Your child will love the illustration details that include spaceships, airplanes, birthday party scenes, clowns with balloons, and much more to delight the eye and trigger conversation and questions. The rhythm of the rhyme will hold parent and toddler's attention. The

S
T
A
G
E
6

variety of vocabulary will stretch your child's language and introduce her to another level of word knowledge.

PARENTESE TIPS AND TALKING POINTS ABOUT THE ILLUSTRATIONS:

- Talk about some of the details in the illustrations, like the restaurant scene in which the boy is sticking breadsticks in his ears, and the girl is putting olives in her nostrils.

- After reading the book several times or more, stop before coming to a rhyming word at the end of a phrase or sentence, and see if your toddler can say the word. For example, if you have read a line that ends in stop, see if your child can find the word at the end of the sentence that rhymes with stop (pop). Recognizing rhyming sounds is a skill that is tested in kindergarten. Children that have been read to on a regular basis have no difficulty recognizing rhyming sounds.

- This book has two major features: the flow of the rhyme and the details of the illustrations to talk about. We recommend that for the first few interactive read-aloud sessions, you go through the book, look at the pictures, and talk about them at your child's pace. Allow your child to get used to the book and get to know the pictures. Then you can start reading the rhyming text from the book with fewer interruptions. When you can read the book straight through your toddler can hear the rhymes and get the meanings.

My Little People Farm
Mi pequeña granja
Large board book
Readers Digest Children's Publishing, 10 pages,
    2003

Book cover: *My Little People Farm*

Not only is this book bilingual (Spanish and English), it has flaps, and teaches a specific concept on each page, like counting, colors, shapes, opposites, and farm animal names. The illustrations are toy-like. Each page has a short rhyme in English and Spanish introducing the concept that is being taught on that page. The rest of the text are labels on, near, or under the flap.

S
T
A
G
E
6

PARENTESE TIPS AND TALKING POINTS ABOUT THE ILLUSTRATIONS:

- Allow your child to select one of his favorite pages in the book. Depending on the page he picks, parent will say, "OK, today we're going to learn about colors." As your child opens the flap that says, "purple," talk to him in complete sentences about what is purple. Say, "the flowers are purple; let's see what's inside. Look, they're fluffy gray bunnies." Even if there is not a lot of text, every time you open a flap, you can talk in complete sentences about the number, color, or shape.

- Even if you're talking about the book in English, you can read the words in Spanish. If you speak Spanish, you can interact with this book entirely in Spanish.

PART III

Practical Tips and Resources

CHAPTER 9

Frequently Asked Questions About Talking and Reading to Babies

As reading specialists, we are often asked the same questions by parents and caregivers. These questions fall into five categories, which we have listed here so that you can go right to the area of your concern. The categories are:

1. Talking to your baby
2. Reading to your baby
3. Speaking more than one language at home
4. Watching television and other screen media
5. Children with special needs

The answers given in this chapter underline the importance of the choices of routines you establish with your baby from the first day, and the effect of these routines on your baby's future. With the birth of a baby, parents' lives change in the interest of giving children the best foundation possible. You will probably change your sleeping and eating schedules, as well as your television viewing habits. Initially, some parents may resist so many changes, but when you consider the degree of influence you have over your baby's growing brain, and the short interval of the first two or three years it takes to form that brain, you will soon realize what a privilege it is to be such a positive force in your child's life.

"It is the environmental engineering and direct input from the parent that helps shape the neurological connections of infants who are later seen as smart, capable, and competent," states William H. Staso, Ph.D., in *Neural Foundations: What Stimulation Your Baby Needs to Become Smart.*[1] As you see the incremental growth in your infant, day-by-day, you will know that your efforts were worth any temporary loss of sleep or other changes in your life.

In the following responses to parents' questions, we not only give our own answers, but also incorporate tips from other parents and experts in language and child development. In the discussions, you will find a variety of parent issues confronting today's parents, including the language ability of the nanny/day care provider, watching television and other screen media, interactive electronic toys, speaking more than one language at home, problems getting a nine-month-old to pay attention to read-alouds, and what to tell friends who don't read to their babies. These and many more questions are addressed in this chapter.

Questions and Answers

Questions about Talking to Your Baby

> *Emotional security may be the number one target for enrichment in infants and toddlers, but language is a close second.*
> Marian Diamond, Ph.D., and Janet Hopson,
> *Magic Trees of the Mind*[2]

Q: We've heard that parents should talk to their babies. My husband and I are not very talkative. Why should we talk to a baby who does not respond or understand?

A: Actually your baby's brain *does* respond by producing dendrite extensions from the neuronal cells. You might even notice your baby's responsive hand, leg, or eye movements when you talk or read to him. Even when your baby is asleep, his brain cells are receptive to language. As William Staso, Ph.D., states in his book, *Neural Foundations: What Stimulation Your Baby Needs to Become Smart:* "Infants should be spoken to as if they understood every word you were saying. In the beginning months your baby will not understand the words you say—but there is much about your intonation patterns and the word sounds that you make that *is* important. Good foundations of language begin shortly after birth."[3]

Talk about what you are doing with your baby. For example, "Is it time to change your diaper? Oh yes, I think we need to change your diaper. Let's go to the changing table and put on a new diaper," etc., etc. When you can't think of anything else to say, this is a good time to reach for a book and begin reading.

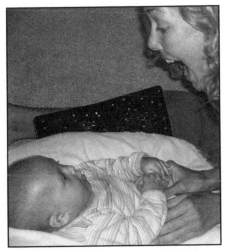

This baby experiences a flood of loving words, not just about books, but about everything she does with mom throughout the day.

Q: When my mother comes to visit our baby, she talks to her in a squeaky, high-pitched voice. Is baby talk good for a baby?

A: This high-pitched singsong is a form of speech heard almost universally around the world, in cultures from Kenya to Canada. This kind of melodic speech is referred to as parentese, motherese, or infant- or child-directed speech. This is not to be confused with "baby talk," which is largely unintelligible (see discussion of parentese in Chapter 2). In their book, *How Babies Talk,* Drs. Golinkoff and Hirsh-Pasek state that this kind of speech helps babies hear the sounds of language more clearly.[4] When using parentese, you exaggerate sounds. You also use shorter sentences and pause longer between utterances.

As a parent, you must remember that you are the linguistic role model for your child. Always try to use the appropriate words for objects and model good language structure. In speaking parentese, you only vary the speed and tone of language. You should not make up or mispronounce words.

Q: My husband and I both work. Our baby will have to go to daycare. What should we look for in searching for quality daycare?

A: Infants go to in-home daycare or a preschool as young as three months. You will need to do your homework, research through your friends and colleagues, and interview the director as well as some of the providers who will be directly involved with your baby. First determine how much one-to-one attention, and how many children besides your own, each adult is responsible for. What are babies spending most of their time doing? Do they spend a lot of time alone, or is someone interacting with and talking to them most of the time? Are there a lot of baby books in sight? Ask about how often someone reads interactively to babies on a one-to-one basis. Stop in unannounced and see the kind of interaction between the providers and other babies. What is the noise level? Is the atmosphere peaceful or hectic? Is there a TV blaring? Your child should never be placed in front of a TV, no matter how "educational."

Q: Do interactive electronic toys help babies learn language and numbers and colors?

A: These so-called educational toys are expensive, and children will only play with them a short time. Once the element of surprise is gone, these toys usually sit ignored on the shelf. Many parents find that their children enjoy playing with regular household items. Some of baby's favorite "toys" are strainers, brooms, mops, pots, pans, spoons, napkins, and cloths for cleaning. Babies enjoy emulating anything that their parents and older siblings do. The most important part of baby's engagement with these "toys" is creative interaction and conversation.

Questions about Reading to Your Baby

> *No wonder experts tell us that children need to hear a thousand stories read aloud before they begin to learn to read for themselves. A thousand!*
>
> Mem Fox, *Reading Magic*[5]

Q: I'm having a hard time reading and talking when I read aloud, because my nine-month-old has started flipping pages and changing books. What should I do?

A: When your baby was younger, you probably chose to read to him when he was fed, rested, and alert. We suggest that at about eight or nine months, you start reading as part of his bedtime routine, because your baby has been fed and has had a warm bath, and you have turned off the television and dimmed the lights. The family is gearing down and beginning to relax in preparation for bedtime. Your baby becomes less energetic when he is winding down. He will be less distracted and more likely to listen to mother's or father's voice.

You will still read at other times of the day, but it may be more challenging. Try different positions, like both of you lying on your backs and looking up at the book. You can also change the focus of your reading. Rather than talking about the pictures in the book, your conversation might turn toward what your baby is doing in relation to the book. For example, "Let's read this book about animals. Look at the duck, quack, quack." As your child grabs the book and goes to the last page, you could say, "So, you want to go to the end of this book. Let's see what animal we can find there. This is the last page. Look, the duck found his mommy!" Then he may grab the book again, turn it upside down, and try turning pages. But whatever he does, you verbalize and are thus pointing out the different parts of the book (concepts of print that are taught at the kindergarten level), including features such as the front and back of the book, the words, the spine, the title, and so forth. By two years of age, children who have been read to since birth know these features readily.

Another example is a nine-month-old who was typically very active during reading time. Parents maintained the reading routine at bedtime, but followed baby's lead by allowing him to carry books from one box to another as mother or dad read to him. When he was learning how to walk, this baby enjoyed standing against a trunk and flipping the pages of his board books as one of his parents read and sat next to him on the floor. The point here is that the interaction with books was maintained during this active stage of the child's development. At one-and-a-half years he was able to settle down and listen to stories for a longer time. For another example of reading under challenging circumstances, see the Chapter 5 example of a mother reading to her eight-month-old twins.

Q: Since I did not start reading to our baby until fourteen months, he's not used to it and doesn't seem interested. How can I get him to take interest and listen?

A: It may take weeks of practice and patience on your part. It's a question of which book, the right time of day, and how you are reading the book. Don't give up. On the other hand, don't "force feed" him books, either. It takes gentle nudging by introducing a variety of books at the right moment and doing it as part of your daily routine. Often boys enjoy truck or train books. Sooner or later, you'll find a book that catches his interest. If he has a box or shelf of books that he has access to, he may, of his own volition, get one and bring it to you. As much as anything he may desire your cuddly closeness when reading. Once he realizes he will win your attention by having you read, he may be hooked.

However, if there are many distractions in your home, such as background TV or video games, your child could be in a state of overstimulation, which doesn't foster reaching for a book. In addition, try different ways of reading the book. In Chapter 2 we discussed ways to dramatize and adjust the text to engage your baby. You don't have to read each word of the book, but tailor the words to what you think your baby would like.

For example, point to or label the objects or creatures, such as the mouse in *Goodnight Moon*. After you have gone through the book several times labeling the creatures, ask your baby, "Where is the mouse?" Soon your baby will be happily pointing to something on each page. "Reading" the book could merely entail asking your baby to find things. You might not read the actual text at all. Eventually, your baby will be engrossed with every word you read as well as your discussions about the illustrations.

To capitalize on this toddler's interests in cars, trucks, and airplanes, uncle and toddler discuss pictures in a book that is too advanced to read, but fun to talk about.

Try to be consistent regarding the time of day when you read, such as before naptime or bedtime. Read on a regular basis, and don't give up just because your baby was not interested the first few times you tried reading. You would not give up if you were teaching your child to ride a bike and he fell down on the first few tries. You would patiently hold him and guide him, time and again, until he was able to ride on his own. It's the same with books!

Q: When is the best time to read to my newborn baby?

A: The best time to read to newborns is anytime, even when they are nursing. Newborns tire easily. If your baby falls asleep, you can keep reading because your voice will continue to comfort him. However, if your baby is experiencing some discomfort due to colic, use your best judgment about whether to continue. Sometimes the sound of your voice and a change in position will soothe their discomforts. See example of father reading to his newborn in Chapter 3.

Q: **What do I tell my friends who wonder why I read to my newborn, when they don't read to their babies?**

A: We suggest you share this brief quote from one of our favorite authors, Jim Trelease: "If a child is old enough to talk to, she is old enough to be read to. It's the same language."[6] You could also tell parents the following: Reading to my baby is just one more way of interacting with him. We cuddle, talk, read, and look at picture books. This is one way of ensuring his language development. Through books

Most parents read to their children at bedtime because it has a calming effect and gets them ready for sleep. Here big brother is doing the reading.

we can experience words and language we would not encounter on a daily basis. Besides getting language, my baby is comforted by my voice and learns a variety of intonations, rhythms, volumes, and pitches. Sitting quietly and reading is one of our favorite times of the day. We will keep our reading routine on into his school years.

Q: **My friends don't read to their babies and have not read the books that support the importance of talking and reading to babies. (These books are listed in the resource section.) How can I share with them the importance of reading to their babies?**

A: One way is to form a book club in which you read not only *Baby Read-Aloud Basics*, but some parts of the other parenting books mentioned in the bibliography at the end of the book. You get together at various intervals and have a book discussion. Since you have read some of these books, you could lead the discussion and bring out some important points. The point of the group would be for parents to give each other support and motivation. You could also share and trade the books you read to your babies. You could combine or alternate reading books for babies and books for moms. You could also work out a system for sharing baby books, and even donating books to churches or preschools in lower socioeconomic areas of your community.

Q: My twenty-three-month-old wants me to read the same book again and again. Is this good?

A: In the same way that babies and toddlers like to hear songs repeatedly, they also like and need to hear books read again and again. Repeated readings help children internalize the language. This is how their hearing becomes refined enough to detect rhymes and rhythms, which helps them acquire and later speak and read their own language. From repeated readings, babies gain meaning and nuances they will draw upon when they become readers.

We have talked to parents whose children have automatically taught themselves how to read at the early age of three. These children had so internalized the language of the books that were read to them repeatedly that they made the link to the actual letters and words on the pages in a way that allowed them to become early readers. Most children who are read to repeatedly as babies will learn to read effortlessly by first grade.

Q: My child only wants to hear Dr. Seuss books. How do I introduce new books?

A: The reason we don't have the wonderful Dr. Seuss books in our "Baby Books at a Glance" sections is that Dr. Seuss books were meant for beginning readers. They have very limited vocabulary in most cases. Babies and toddlers have vocabularies that grow each day, and will be supported by books that use a variety of vocabulary words. We want our babies to hear rich vocabularies from books. Many adults know only about the famous Dr. Seuss books, and think wrongly that babies can only understand a simple vocabulary. While it's fine to include Dr. Seuss books, with their humorous and engaging illustrations, in your read-aloud times, don't neglect the wide range of other baby and toddler books available.

If your baby doesn't seem to enjoy some of your other selections, keep trying until you find one that captures his attention. Be sure to dramatize, as we suggest in Chapter 2. Make faces, sounds, and gestures. Make a game out of your reading sessions. Include some of your child's trucks or toys, which may look like some of the illustrations.

Questions about Speaking More Than One Language at Home

> *There is considerable evidence that quality literacy instruction in the native language facilitates overall academic achievement and the development of English literacy skills."*
> Bertha Pérez and Maria E. Guzmán,
> *Learning in Two Worlds*[7]

Q: My husband and I are native Spanish speakers. We want our children to do well in school. Our English isn't as good as our Spanish. Should we try to speak and read English to our children?

A: It's best to speak and read to your children in the language in which you feel most comfortable, even if it is not the language taught in schools. Your children need to hear lots of vocabulary and lots of good language. Better that your children should hear good Spanish than poor English. There is some evidence that children with a well-developed home language will successfully learn other languages and do well in school. Children who have not heard enough language, no matter what that language is, usually struggle learning to read.

This mother reads to her toddler in Spanish. A good foundation in the home language will help in learning a second language.

So it is not *which* language that matters, but the amount and quality of the language children hear between birth and two years of age. If children's home language is filled with rich descriptions from books and explanations from parents, they will have more language to be able to question, investigate, and make sense of their environment. The more language children hear, the more intelligent they become. They will become good communicators and successful in reading, math, and the arts.

Participate as a family in English language community events, such as weekly library read-alouds, activities at your place of worship, playgroups, and sports events. Try to enroll your toddler a few days a week in a preschool where the teachers and other children speak English. Your children's strong Spanish language foundation along with their early experiences in the English-speaking community will help them become bilingual as well as succeed in school.

Q: **Why does having a strong knowledge of the primary language of your parents make it easier to learn a second language?**

A: Basically the more words you learn, the more words you can speak. If you see or hear the word *blue* in English, and if you speak French, you can relate *blue* to *bleu* in French. The brain connections have already been developed using the home language. Concepts learned in one language easily transfer to another language. If your baby didn't have the necessary concepts, he would be held back intellectually. Think of the amount of things we explain to our babies in the first years of life that contribute to the development of brain connections. It doesn't matter from which language the brain connections come.

Q: **We speak French at home, and I worry that when my child goes to kindergarten, she won't understand what the teacher is saying.**

A: If you are living in a predominantly English-speaking country, for example, your child will learn English as soon as she becomes part of the larger community. Learning English will be easiest for those children who have the largest vocabularies in their home language. Young children have the ability to easily learn new vocabulary. They have the motivation because they want to become part of the social group and are not shy about speaking a new language. To make the transition to kindergarten easier for you child, expose her to English by associating as much as possible with English speakers outside of the home in English-speaking community activities and by enrolling her in English-speaking preschool.

As teachers, we have worked with children whose home language is not English and who have higher language ability in English than native English speakers who have not been spoken to and read to enough at home. These children do better in school than their native English-speaking counterparts.

Q: **If we speak a different language at home, how long will it take my child to speak English (or the majority language), once he starts kindergarten?**

A: It depends on the following conditions:

- The amount of language and reading your child was exposed to from birth (in any language)
- Your child's involvement in the English-speaking community, such as sports or religious groups
- Your child's attendance in English-speaking daycare or an English-speaking preschool with a low student/teacher ratio and access to books
- Your child's exposure to older siblings and family members who speak English (or whatever the dominant language is of the country you are living in)

We have seen children from Spanish-speaking homes that can read English text at grade level after only one year of kindergarten, if most of these conditions have been met.

Q: **My wife and I both work. We have a nanny who takes care of our three-month-old baby. Our concern is that the nanny does not speak English very well, and we don't know if she has a strong vocabulary in her own language. What should we do?**

A: We know from research (see Chapter 1) that babies need to hear an extraordinary amount of language from an articulate adult. It does not matter what language it is. If your nanny has good language skills in French, for example, she could speak in her language to your baby. Your baby will effortlessly acquire another language while the brain is most absorbent and primed to learn language. Any good language input creates growth of brain cell connections. If your nanny doesn't have a high vocabulary in her native language or your language, you might want to consider finding someone who has more language skills. If your nanny was merely an aide and you or someone with good language ability were home most of the day with the baby and did most of the talking, your baby would not be missing out on a rich language experience. If you're not comfortable with your baby hearing another language, then you should find a nanny with good English language skills.

Q: **My husband is Japanese, and I am a native English speaker. We want our child to know both English and Japanese and grow up to be bilingual. My Japanese isn't fluent, and my husband's English isn't fluent, but we communicate in English. What should we do?**

A: Since your husband is a fluent Japanese speaker, he should speak and read to your baby in Japanese, and you, as a fluent English speaker, should speak and read to your baby in English. It is important that your baby hears both languages from the moment of birth. At birth, babies' brains are capable of learning any language. For the first eight months, babies focus on the *rhythm* of the languages they are exposed to. At eight months, babies begin to focus on the *sounds* of their own home language (or languages) and lose the ability to hear and produce sounds in other languages.[8] Hearing the rhythm and sounds of your home languages before age one will help ensure that your baby will be able to speak these languages.

We are not saying that your child will never be able to learn another language, but most of us have experienced how difficult it is to learn another language as young or older adults. After one year of age, the brain prunes away the excess brain connections used to detect all the world's languages so that a baby can specialize in the language or languages heard in the home.

In addition, your baby needs to continue hearing and interacting in both languages in order to develop and maintain those languages. Your husband could talk and read to your baby in Japanese, and you could talk and read in English. Once your baby goes to preschool, he will hear more English than Japanese. As a result, your husband and any relatives who speak Japanese will need to continue to interact in that language, or English will take over. Your child will hear social language everyday from the interaction with your husband and his family. However, if your child is going to maintain Japanese after he has started school (and is immersed in English), your husband will have to make a conscious effort to read to him in Japanese to enlarge his vocabulary to include more "rare" (see Chapter 1) and academic vocabulary. If English does eventually overtake Japanese in early childhood, your child will be able to return to it again more easily later in life because of having heard it in his first years of life.[9]

Q: How can I encourage our nanny to read to our baby in English when she can't speak English very well and her vocabulary is limited?

A: If your nanny doesn't feel comfortable reading in English, an alternative would be to "read" the illustrations speaking her own language. She could make up stories based on the illustrations using the language in which she is comfortable. Your baby will learn the rhythm and pronunciation of another language, something he or she will be thankful for in future years. Your nanny could also point to the objects and give them labels in her language. Objects like water, book, boy, or girl can be great fun in another language when the whole family gets involved. Talk to your nanny and explain how and when she can read books. Provide her with books that lend themselves to labeling common objects.

Q: **I'm Chinese and my husband is Canadian. I sing nursery rhymes from my childhood to my three-month-old. I now want to start reading to my baby in Chinese. My husband, who speaks English, thinks hearing two languages will confuse our baby.**

A: Babies under six months can hear the sounds of all the earth's languages, sounds that later become impossible to pronounce, like the French "r" for English speakers and the English "r" for Chinese speakers. There is a window of opportunity in the first year to perceive and maintain these and many other sounds. If you want your baby eventually to be able to speak Chinese without an English accent, it is important that you continue to sing, read, and talk to your baby. Your baby will also need to pick up the Chinese word order (grammar and syntax) from hearing it.

Will your baby be confused by also hearing English from your husband? Babies's brains are very pliable and absorbent. They can pick up more than one language at once. However, when he first starts talking, your child may interchange some words of both languages because he isn't sure which words go with which language. But as he grows older, he will become aware of who is speaking which language, and he will figure out how to separate them. Even if at the beginning he uses two languages in the same sentence, your child internalizes the correct grammar for each language. By the time your child reaches school age, he'll have figured out in which situations to use each language and with which people. Make sure that once your child is in school, you continue to read and talk to him in Chinese. He needs to learn the value of bilingualism in order to speak to his relatives. If you can travel to China to visit relatives or maintain relationships with the Chinese community in your area, your child will see the value in knowing more than one language. When he grows up he'll be grateful for his language ability as well as knowledge of his cultural heritage.

Questions about Watching Television

> *It does not take the orphanage scene from* David Copperfield *to qualify as an impoverished environment. All it takes is a toddler sitting alone and passive for hours in front of the television set, dreaming eyes of wonder glazed over, imagination shelved, exploratory energy on hold. Then throw in a bowl of potato chips and soda. . . .*
>
> Marian Diamond, Ph.D. and Janet Hopson,
> *Magic Trees of the Mind*[10]

Q: **How long should I leave my five-month-old in front of the television? She seems to like to look at it.**

A: Some parents might think that placing babies in front of the bright-colored screen will entertain them and maybe even teach them some vocabulary. One parent told us that his six-month-old loved to watch Sponge Bob on TV. For babies under ten months, the television screen is just a confusing blur. It serves no purpose. During their first year of life, it is crucial for babies to listen to and be actively involved in language face-to-face with a caring adult. Language fosters a baby's ability to think and to solve problems as well as control his emotions. During this time, it is important for you to respond actively to his vocalizations and facial expressions. The two-dimensional picture on the television screen lacks the ability to interact with a baby. Putting babies in front of the television at an early age does not stimulate them. Furthermore, it sets a precedent for future behavior.

Watching television is a habit that is easily formed and very difficult to break. The American Academy of Pediatrics suggests that parents not expose their children to television before the age of two.[11] (See Chapter 10.)

Q: **My older children watch TV. How can I prevent our one-year-old from watching with them?**

A: Anyone who has any doubts about the negative effects of television on children should read Jim Trelease's Chapter 8 on television from his highly recommended *The Read-Aloud Handbook*. Trelease mentions numerous studies that point to the addictive nature of television, calling it the "plug in" drug.[12] Marian Diamond and Janet Hopson, in their book, *Magic Trees of the Mind,* discuss the endless hours children lose by sitting passively instead of engaging actively in other activities.[13] Children could be outdoors, playing games with toys, or pretending. Almost any activity is more stimulating to the brain than watching television. It's important to limit the amount of time your children watch TV and monitor what they watch. While your older children are watching television, you can take advantage of this time to talk and read to your baby. You may find that one or more of the children watching television will join you as you read to your baby.

Q: **My children are so used to watching TV. What else could they do, instead?**

A: The issue of children spending too much time watching television and other screen media has become a huge problem for parents. The Kaiser study, released in October 2003, found that children age zero to six spend as much time with television, computers, and video games as playing outside. Children in "heavy" TV households are less likely to read. Two-thirds of children (65 percent) live in homes where the TV is left on at least half the time or more. One third (36 percent) live in homes where the TV is "always" on. The children from this latter group are less likely than other children to be able to read at ages four through six. Yet, according to the study, almost all parents (96 percent) consider books "very important" to children's intellectual development, while two-thirds (66 percent) consider books the most important when compared to other media or toys.[14]

There are no easy solutions to the presence of television in the home. We are not suggesting there is any right way or one way to approach TV watching. "Just saying no" doesn't solve the problem, and there is no reason for individual parents to feel guilty, as it is an issue that all of us, including the creators of children's programming and related toys, must address. Chief among the issues is the violence that permeates TV programs, computer and video games, and media-linked toys. The book *Remote Control Childhood, Combating the Hazards of Media Culture* by Diane E. Levin thoughtfully explores the problem.[15] In addition to *Remote Control Childhood*, parents can consult *365 TV-Free Activities You Can Do with Your Child*, by Steve and Ruth Bennett.[16] (For children under age two, see our Chapter 10 for language activities to do with your baby instead of watching TV.)

You may also start a discussion with your toddler by reading *Fix It* by David McPhail.[17] This little book is suitable for age two and under. It features a little bear, Emma, who got up early to watch television, but it didn't work. Emma becomes more and more upset as no one could fix the television. Eventually her mother consoled her by reading Emma a book. When the television was finally repaired, Emma was uninterested. She was too busy with her book.

Q: Does television help babies learn new words?

A: Television cannot provide the necessary word input. Besides the fact that television offers a low level of vocabulary, babies need a one-to-one relationship with a parent or caregiver who is personally talking and reading to them.

The vital language interaction and exploration between you and your precious baby cannot be accomplished through any electronic means such as television, computer, or video, no matter what the educational quality. Babies need face-to-face, one-to-one human interaction in which parent and child develop a synchronizing dance of responses to one another's facial expressions, voices (using parentese—see Chapter 2), and gestures. This kind of feedback is necessary for providing healthy human relationships where babies learn to pick up ("read") important cues that signal emotional states. The type of language heard on television is not that of a mother speaking directly to the developmental needs of her baby. Teachers know that children who watch too much television are often poor students.

Questions about Children with Special Needs

> *A young man with Down syndrome spoke to a University class during the 1970s. One student asked him, "What did your parents do for you that you appreciate the most?" His answer was, "They taught me to read. When you can read, you can go anywhere and do anything."*
>
> Patricia Logan Oelwein,
> *Magic: Teaching Reading to Children with Down Syndrome*[18]

Q: Can babies with Down syndrome, chromosomal disorders, cerebral palsy, or any other special needs be helped by being read to?

A: We recommend reading to all babies, as long as they seem comforted by it. While we were working on this book, a wonderful teacher who attended one of our workshops recommended *Cushla and Her Books,* by

Dorothy Butler.[19] Cushla was afflicted from birth in the early 1970s with multiple handicaps caused by chromosomal damage. Her doctors assumed she was also mentally retarded. She spent many weeks hospitalized, and doctors recommended she be institutionalized. In spite of Cushla's discouraging prognosis, her parents talked and read to her unceasingly from the age of four months. Cushla's parents started reading to her as a way to pass the hours at the hospital and during her many sleepless nights. But the reading became a habit, and as a result, Cushla's language and cognition developed way beyond the expectations of her doctors. She eventually tested above average in intelligence and social adjustment. By the age of six, Cushla could read fluently, although she still had vision, hearing, and some physical disabilities.

Cushla's story is not the only case in which reading to a child from infancy can make a miraculous difference. Jim Trelease has told Cushla's story in each edition of his *The Read-Aloud Handbook,* in the hope of inspiring parents of children with difficulties of any kind. He received letters from the parents of a child with Down syndrome and one with a brain disorder. Both sets of parents were given the grim prognosis that their children would not talk and would be severely retarded. After reading *The Read-Aloud Handbook,* the parents put their children on a steady "diet" of read-alouds many times a day from early infancy. Both children eventually went to school, read at grade level, and loved books.[20] These remarkable children and their persistent parents illustrate the power of reading in the development of important early brain cell connections and pathways.

Q: I have read to my child since birth, but he had difficulties with reading throughout first grade. He is now in second grade and has been diagnosed with a reading disability. We are a family of readers. Why didn't all the read-alouds help my son acquire reading skills?

A: There are many reasons why some children have reading difficulties in spite of the fact that you did everything you could to ensure your child's success. Let us assure you that it is even more important that you read to your child when there is a chance of a reading difficulty. We hope you will continue to read to him. Your son will have a great vocabulary because of your read-alouds, and he will succeed, in spite of this setback.

Reading difficulties can be experienced by anyone, regardless of IQ or the parents' educational level. By reading to your child, you are still providing him with knowledge, vocabulary, and a love of books. In time, with intervention from speech and language and reading specialists, your child will develop the strategies and skills necessary to becoming a competent reader. Occasionally there are students who have severe disabilities that require other means of input, such as computers, tapes, and CDs. Nevertheless, the advanced vocabulary, knowledge, and love of books inspired by being read to from birth will make all the difference in a student's quest for success and self-esteem. When parents read to their babies and toddlers, they are giving love and support—the foundation to a successful life.

CHAPTER 10

Fun Activities and Tips to Manage TV and Make a Language-Rich Home

In order for babies to hear enough language, parents and other family members need to give babies as much one-to-one, face-to-face conversation and attention as possible. How do you accomplish this in the noisy, busy world that has invaded your private home spaces?

The key is rearranging your family or living room space into a *Reader's Nest*, whose focus is language and reading promoting activities. This means that you not make your television the center of attention, or a media shrine surrounded by shelves of videos. It means making tubs, baskets, and bookshelves full of books the focus, and placing the television in a discreet corner or cabinet with doors that close when not in use.

Making your Home a Reader's Nest

There are three changes you can make in your family living space that will help you achieve your daily schedule while providing your baby with an abundance of reading and talking opportunities.

Read-Aloud Chair

Determine the areas where you spend the most time as a family. These could be the nursery, the master bedroom, or the family or living room. Provide a comfortable read-aloud chair in the place you spend the most time with your baby. The place could change as your baby grows. The chair should be in a clutter-free zone, with books close by. You don't need to buy a special chair. Your read-aloud chair can be your nursing glider, a favorite old rocker, or couch. What's important is the daily routine of giving one-to-one attention to your child with books in a familiar place where you are both comfortable

Your child will associate the intimacy of the cuddly reading chair with the fun of read-alouds. From the time of baby's birth this will be the place you mostly go to enjoy cozy read-aloud time. It will be the heart of your home's Reader's Nest. Though you may read in several areas, including the floor or bed, your child's favorite place will always be your lap!

Baby's Portable Book Bins, Baskets, and Bookshelves

Baskets, tubs, or shelves of books need to be available in all areas where you read to baby, so that you'll never have to search for a book. A few quality books for each stage in your baby's development are essential to your Reader's Nest. As your baby grows, she'll begin to have favorite books. If you place those books in a basket or tub, you can easily move from one area to another. You can use existing bookshelves. Clear off the bottom two shelves, so that by seven or eight months your crawling baby can gain access to the books, even if it means pulling them out and playing with them. Babies will search out and recognize books that have been read to

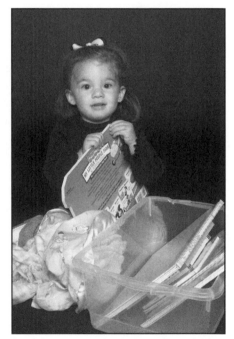

At eighteen months, baby enjoys picking out books and pointing to the pictures.

them repetitively. Soon after they can sit up, and before they begin to talk, they will be picking out favorite books and handing them to you to read.

One parent told us how she keeps board books, animal magazines, and toy catalogues on the bottom shelf so her toddler can reach them. She doesn't care if her toddler rips magazines. She keeps other favorite bedtime books with soft covers or pages that could easily rip low enough on shelves for the toddler to see and point to, but just out of reach. If her toddler points to one of the out of reach books, an adult will come and read it to her. But when her toddler is on her own she can reach, look at, and play with any of the durable baby books and dispensable magazines.

Language Play Area

This part of your Reader's Nest is an area that you will set up in the family room near the kitchen so that you can prepare meals while talking and keeping an eye on your baby. The purpose of this area is to make a safe, TV-free, language-promoting play area for your baby. All you have to have is a safe area away from electrical wires and outlets, where you can provide various toys, books, and items from around the house. One way to keep your baby's interest is by putting some toys and books in this area and every several days exchanging them for some other toys and books she hasn't seen in a couple of weeks. At the end of this chapter you'll find activities for this area. These activities support your baby's language development and give you alternatives to placing baby in front of the TV.

Television and Media

Parents instinctively know that their babies and toddlers need to be read to. A recent Kaiser Family Study tells us that 96 percent of parents know that books are more important for their children than any electronic media.[1] Yet these same studies show that babies are subjected to more and more TV and other screen media, even though the American Academy of Pediatrics recommends that children below the age of two should not watch TV.[2]

The growing use of TV, videos, DVDs, digital phones, and computers may be the biggest obstacle to babies achieving good language development today. Most learning problems are caused by poor language development. Here are a few of the many statistics that tell us we need to manage our children's TV and other media watching more closely:

- The increasing number of ADD (attention deficit disorder) children has paralleled the increasing number of hours spent in front of various screen media. A recent study has found excessive TV watching to be a major cause of ADD.[3]

- Studies show that by first grade, children have already watched an average of 6,000 hours of TV. American one-year-olds spend an average of six hours a week watching TV. Two-year-olds spend an average of twenty-seven hours a week watching TV.[4]
- Ten hours per week of TV watching is shown to negatively affect academic achievement.[5]
- Many parents spend an average of no more than five minutes of quality time with their child each day.[6]

We're not advocating throwing out the television and other media. Most of us know that television seems to be everywhere, and when we do watch it, we can't seem to pull ourselves away from it. However, we'll do heroic acts for our babies and grandchildren. The above statistics will help parents acknowledge the damage excessive television watching can do to our baby's delicately wired, absorbent, and vulnerable neurological network. The following suggestions and tips will help parents ensure that new baby gets an abundant amount of daily, one-to-one, personal loving language input instead of impersonal, language-deficient, digital input.

Babies zero to two should not be subjected to television or videos/DVDs. But the fact is that the average one-year-old is watching at least six hours of television per week. Nannies, caretakers, and grandparents need to be instructed that children under two should not be watching screen media. Instead of television, show them how to use some of the play activities highlighted in this chapter appropriate for their developmental age.

Once babies are allowed to use television as a form of entertainment, they will be less likely to entertain themselves with toys and books as well as objects found around the house. Television is habit forming, and by the time babies get to be age two, they will already be addicted. Ask yourself, "What is my child not doing while the television mesmerizes her?" Look at the "Television versus Read-Aloud" chart below to see how your baby's brain is not being challenged when watching television. Creative play with blocks or even ordinary household items like plastic lids or wooden spoons promote stimulation that is healthy for a baby's developing brain. Watching television or video should only be used as a last resort for babies before age two. Even older children who are used to watching television will rediscover their toys and other more creative activities if television is not an option.

Do you leave the TV on, but have it muted? Some parents think the TV really isn't on if it's muted. If the TV image is in the background, you will periodically shift your gaze back and forth from your baby's eyes to the TV image. You are teaching your baby how to be distracted, how not to give 100 percent of your attention. Between birth and age two, your baby learns everything about attention and social interaction from parents. So even the image of a muted TV is an unwanted distraction that detracts from attention span and social development.

Do your children have TVs in their rooms? Experts recommend that the TV should be in the family room so that children are not isolated and parents know the amount and content of TV watched. If your children are already accustomed to their own TV, they will initially protest the removal of TV from their bedrooms. Involve your whole family in changing their TV habits. Explain what you have learned about the effects on the brain of excessive TV watching. If you are a first-time parent, take a look at your own TV watching habits and adjust them for the good of your baby.

Children do not gain vocabulary from television. Children's books have fifty percent more rare words than adult prime-time television.[7] Take a look at the "TV Watching versus Reading Aloud" chart below to see how your baby's brain is not being challenged when watching television.

TV Watching vs. Reading Aloud

TV Watching	Reading Aloud
Discourages problem-solving skills	Encourages problem-solving skills
No control over fast pace	Pace controlled by reader/listener
High visual stimulation, frenetic pace	Listener generates own internal stimulation
No person-to-person dialogue	Interactive dialogue with real person
Passive brain in sleep state	Active brain in alert state
No questions, answers, conversation	Frequent questioning, conversation
Encourages short attention span	Encourages long attention span
Antisocial, no relating to others	Lots of discussion and interaction
Low vocabulary level	High vocabulary level
Questionable content, violence, ads	Age-appropriate, parent-selected content
Can encourage ADD (attention deficit disorder)	Helps prevent ADD
Discourages language development	Encourages language development

May not reflect parent values	Word and book choices reflect parent values
Does not teach left-to-right eye movements	Teaches left-to-right eye movements
Does not teach that print carries a message	Teaches concept that print carries a message

Since children who watch ten hours or more of TV a week are at risk for poor academic achievement, select your favorite programs, videos/DVDs, and make sure viewing time is below ten hours per week. Adults can record and watch their programs after children go to sleep. Adult programs (such as news) should not be on when children are present. Even if you think a baby won't understand, you're setting the stage for having the TV on, and your emotional reactions are absorbed by your baby's sensitive nervous system.

Use the following guidelines to help prioritize your TV/video/DVD favorites and reduce your family's viewing time:

- Preselect the programs for the week.
- Reduce TV/DVD viewing to no more than ten hours a week.
- Choose videos/DVDs over programs with ads.
- Limit the number of channels available to reduce exposure to violence.
- Remove TV from children's bedrooms.
- Do not watch TV with adult content while baby and children are present.
- Use TV as last recourse. Use language promoting play activities (see below).

Language Building Activities for Babies from Birth to Two

The following are a sampling of learning activities that will help you accomplish chores such as preparing meals without using TV as a babysitter. We refer to these activities as play, because babies learn through constructive play activities. Once you try some of these activities, you will think of many others. Sometimes you might accidentally discover everyday items that bring your child fun and entertainment. Friends will give you new ideas too. Most of the activities are for Stages Five and Six when babies are most active and parents are most tempted to place baby in front of a television. All of the following activities will benefit your baby's language development as well as promote bonding and attachment.

Safety and close proximity to baby is always a priority for activities in the early years. Any toy that you make or use from materials or objects around your home should be closely inspected to make sure that there are no loose parts that could result in a choking hazard or any type of injury. Babies under age two need to be supervised at all times. When baby cries or becomes fussy, attend to his needs immediately. A rapid response time to baby's needs is crucial for overall trust and sense of security. Remember, you can't spoil a baby.

When babies have had enough of any of the following activities, they will let you know. With a little preparation and planning, these activities will give you some time to get a few important things done while insuring that your baby gets needed stimulation without getting hooked on TV. If both parents in your household work, you can share these activities with your baby's caretakers, so they are aware that you want your baby to be involved in language building activities instead of being placed in front of a television.

Stages One to Two: Ages Birth to Four Months

During these first two stages babies sleep a lot, thus leaving parents a little more free time than at later stages. The activities you'll find here are for babies who are nonmobile, and need to be close to you, yet leave your hands free to get a few things done around the house.

ACTIVITY: Work and Wear
SKILLS: Language development, bonding
WHAT YOU NEED: A wearable sling or baby-secure front pack
PREPARATION: Secure baby into a front pack or sling
DESCRIPTION: Wear your baby while you sweep, vacuum, fold laundry, grocery shop, rake leaves, dust, do computer work, write checks, or any activity where you can keep baby with you. The important part is to talk to your baby about everything you are doing so that she is soothed by your voice and movements and can absorb language for later use. Your baby will feel secure and loved right next to your body.

ACTIVITY: Cook and Coo
SKILLS: Language development, bonding
WHAT YOU NEED: Car seat

PREPARATION: Place your baby in a car seat on a counter away from the edge, or place her near where you will be working in the kitchen away from any heat source. You could also place baby on the floor or kitchen table.

DESCRIPTION: Think of a TV cooking personality like Martha Stewart or Emeril and talk your way through everything you do: "First we put in the flour, then we add a dash of salt," etc. Vocalize everything you do. Look at your baby and use parentese, dramatizing with exaggerated actions and an animated variety of voice tones. Talk about the sounds of the mixer, the pouring of liquids, and the grinding of the sifter, etc. Your baby will probably respond by making cooing sounds, and you can answer and interact accordingly. In this way your baby will hear thousands of words and be entertained while you cook a meal for the family.

ACTIVITY: Look and Learn

SKILLS: Language and visual development

WHAT YOU NEED: Pinwheel toy or balloons

PREPARATION: Stick a pinwheel or balloons in a potted plant outside a sliding glass door or window, so the pinwheel will spin or balloons will bob in the wind. Place baby in car seat inside the window or door so she can view the objects. Babies at these early stages need to be close to objects to see clearly. Rotating ceiling fans also captivate baby's attention at these early stages.

DESCRIPTION: Occasionally, as you go about your chores, get at eye level with baby and talk about the balloons, pinwheel, or ceiling fan. "Look, see the pinwheel spinning?"

ACTIVITY: Sound and Sight Gallery

SKILLS: Language, motor, and visual development

WHAT YOU NEED: Activity gym of your own objects found around the house (such as plastic clothespins, clothesline, little cloth toys, rattles, bells, colorful ribbons, or family photo close-ups of faces).

PREPARATION: Use activity gym if you have one. You can exchange the hanging objects on gym to create new interests for your baby. You can also make up your own Sound and Sight Gallery. Tie or attach items to a clothesline with plastic clothespins and string across a playpen, crib, or between two chairs or table legs. Make sure it's close enough for baby to focus on. Take precaution to stretch the line tightly enough so that it won't be a strangling hazard. Take precaution that items are securely attached and won't fall on baby's face.

DESCRIPTION: As you go about your chores, occasionally bat items to make them move and jingle and say a few words to comfort and let baby know you are nearby.

Stages Three and Four: Ages Four to Twelve Months

Between four and twelve months your baby will become more mobile, requiring a watchful eye at all times. Before your baby begins to crawl, she may roll or scoot off the blanket play area. One way to deal with this is to create little barriers with pillows or furniture—making defined, safe play areas filled with baby's toys. Use firm pillows from a couch or purchase foam blocks covered in vinyl or fabric. The activities presented for these two stages require you to be in close proximity to your baby, but not right beside her.

ACTIVITY: Tumble and Talk
SKILLS: Language and motor development, bonding, balance, coordination
WHAT YOU NEED: Large bed or soft carpeted area and pillows, dad or other playful adult
PREPARATION: When you need to take care of some household chores, enlist dad to play and tumble with baby on bed or soft carpet. Dads naturally play with babies in a more roughhouse manner, which may initially make moms nervous. It's important to allow dad to have some alone time with baby from the beginning so that he can bond in his own way with his child. Though moms may wince at the slightly rough play with baby, it's actually beneficial as long as all safety precautions are taken. Make sure baby's head is supported, she isn't shaken, and she enjoys the activity. Any of these activities can be accompanied by made-up chants or those found in rhyming books in Chapter 6.
DESCRIPTION: The following play activities are part of a repertoire of Tumble and Talk play that comes naturally to most dads:

- *Swimming:* Place baby on her back on the bed, grasping both legs at the ankles and feet and gently pull back and forth as if kicking and stroking in the water. Usually this is done with rhythm while dad may chant something like "swimming, swimming in the water."

- *Push-Ups:* Dad lies on his back on bed and hoists baby above him, moving baby up and down, back and forth, face to face. This will naturally bring about chanting or talking.

- *Airplane:* This position can soothe babies who are colicky or teething. Hold baby so that she or he is facing the floor. One of dad's arms is positioned in between legs supporting baby's tummy and chest. The other hand rests on baby's back, in a kind of football hold. Dad walks around pretending baby is an airplane, making wavy motions and airplane sounds.

- *Obstacle Course:* Dad places pillows on the floor and coaxes baby to wiggle and crawl (after six months of age) over and around piles of pillows. Sometimes a tempting toy as a goal helps baby attempt a new challenge.

ACTIVITY: Baby Tether Ball
SKILLS: Language, visual, and motor development
WHAT YOU NEED: Bouncing ball or plastic beach ball that hangs above baby from ceiling or doorway
PREPARATION: Attach lightweight tetherball or beach ball on a string from ceiling or doorway above baby. Place baby on the floor near where parent is working. Place baby so that ball is above tummy area so she has to reach for ball. At this stage babies are very active and will first gaze at ball, and then try to touch it with hands and feet.
DESCRIPTION: Gently show how to bat ball with arms and legs. Ask questions. "Can you hit the ball with your feet or hands?" Start the ball moving, and once baby is engaged, watching ball move back and forth, you may go about what you have to do, but at the same time keep an eye on baby.

ACTIVITY: Maraca Music Makers
SKILLS: Language, listening, and motor development, cause and effect
WHAT YOU NEED: Plastic spice jars, baby food, or water bottles filled with dried beans or rice, Elmer's glue
PREPARATION: Gather and wash containers and fill with various contents, seal the bottles securely with Elmer's glue. Place containers on blanket or floor where baby can reach them. At these stages babies will be putting everything in their mouths. Make sure there are no labels or any sharp edges. Soaking bottles in soapy, warm water will loosen the labels so they can be easily removed.
DESCRIPTION: Sit with your baby and show her how to manipulate, shake, or roll containers. Talk to your baby about the sounds or actions. The

plastic medicine bottle with the rubber dropper lid is pleasing for babies when teething.

ACTIVITY: Bang and Babble

SKILLS: Language, listening, and motor development, cause and effect

WHAT YOU NEED: Plastic and wooden spoons, pots, pans, strainers, and bowls made out of different unbreakable materials with no sharp edges or pieces that can fall off. Colored blocks are also good for this activity.

PREPARATION: Gather kitchen utensils in a plastic tub or container and place within your baby's reach on a blanket or floor near where you will be working in the kitchen or other part of house.

DESCRIPTION: Sit with your baby on a mat or blanket on the floor and show her how to play with items. For example, take the wooden spoon and bang on the metal pot or pan. Using a bowl or pot with a lid, pretend you are making soup with the blocks and mixing with the spoon. Babies love putting things in containers and then taking them out again. All the while keep up a steady stream of talk back and forth with your baby, responding to her delighted smiles and coos. Once baby seems involved, you can continue your household duties, while keeping an eye on baby as you're working. When your baby is able to crawl and stand, you can put some of these objects in a drawer or lower shelf in the kitchen (away from stove) so that baby can play in the kitchen, emulating cooking, while you work.

Twelve-month-old on the kitchen floor is pretending to make soup like mommy.

ACTIVITY: Water Bottle Bling Bling

SKILLS: Language, motor, and visual development

WHAT YOU NEED: Plastic water or soda bottles with caps, food coloring, light corn syrup, metallic confetti-type glitter of different sparkly shapes and colors, colored marbles, little plastic figures, any sparkly objects you can find, water, Elmer's glue to permanently seal bottle closed.

PREPARATION: Collect used, clean plastic water or soda bottles that are in good condition. Soak overnight in warm, soapy water to remove labels. Fill bottles 3/4 full of corn syrup. Add a small handful of confetti and top the bottle off with water. Add food coloring, different kinds of confetti glitter, and other sparkly objects to make each bottle different. Make sure caps are sealed with Elmer's glue and that the glue is dry so lids can't be pulled off. You can make a couple of bottles, and slowly add to your collection as you find interesting sparkly objects.

DESCRIPTION: Sit with your baby on a mat or blanket on the floor and show her how to play, shake, and move bottles around so baby can see the bling bling (sparkling items) and understands the cause and effect. Talk about the colors, glitter shapes, and everything you see happening in the bottles. Show baby how to roll the bottles around the play area. She can also stand them up like bowling pins and roll a ball toward the bottles to knock them over.

Stages Five and Six: Ages Twelve Months to Two Years

During these stages your baby is acquiring new vocabulary at a rapid rate. Your child is absorbing every word you say and read. The more these words are heard, the faster your toddler will learn them and eventually be able to say them. Your toddler not only imitates your vocabulary, but your actions. If you turn on the TV, for example, during dinner preparation, your child will expect it on at the same time every day. However, if you involve your toddler in the following language-building activities, he will expect these instead of the language-deficient television.

ACTIVITY: What's Inside?

SKILLS: Language development, problem solving, and motor movements

WHAT YOU NEED: Different size empty containers, like used diaper wipe containers or shoe boxes; baby toys such as rattles, balls, and stuffed animals; colorful wrapping paper; paper shopping bags; and books. You can also use small paper lunch bags instead of wrapping paper.

PREPARATION: Put a few toys in boxes found around the house. Loosely wrap several objects in bright paper (don't use ribbons or strings, just paper). The objects might be baby's favorite toys, wooden spoons, rattles, plastic cups, balls, books, or rubber ducks. You can also put some of these same objects into a small paper lunch bag.

DESCRIPTION: Sit with your baby and show her how to take off the wrapping paper and pull out the toys while asking her, "What's inside?" As you pull objects out of the wrapper or small paper bags, say, "It's your little white bunny with soft, long ears," for example. Use words like open, close, inside, outside, top, bottom, as well as textures like soft, round, and sounds like crinkly paper and tearing paper. Keep changing wrapped objects to add new interest. If done with small paper bags, this activity can be taken to appointments or other places outside of home to keep your baby busy.

ACTIVITY: Parent's Little Helper

SKILLS: Language development, social, and motor movements

WHAT YOU NEED: Toy versions of household cleaning items, such as brooms, mops, rakes, and adult dust pans, dish rags, sponges, and plastic dishes.

PREPARATION: Provide the toy version or actual tool of whatever you're going to be using around the house or in your work at home.

DESCRIPTION: If you're mixing something, give your child a bowl and spoon to imitate your actions. If you're sweeping, allow your child to sweep. Toddlers also enjoy toy shopping carts into which they can put cans out of the cupboard and deposit them in the living room. This keeps toddler busy while parent is cooking. Toddlers also love to clean surfaces with a wet sponge. To keep the mess to a minimum, the wet sponge activity can be done in a high chair. There is so much dialogue that can take place around these activities that will help your toddler acquire vocabulary. Verbs such as wiping, sweeping, dusting, cleaning, raking, shopping, typing, and writing, as well as color and number words, will add to your child's developing vocabulary. *Caution*: Most household cleaners contain toxic substances. A child is just as happy with a spray bottle with plain water or a wet sponge.

ACTIVITY: Tower Talk

SKILLS: Language and motor development, problem solving, shape and size discrimination

WHAT YOU NEED: Wooden or plastic blocks, stackable plastic containers, cereal boxes, or any safe objects that can be built into a tower and knocked down.

PREPARATION: Assemble a box full of blocks and other items that can be used by you and your toddler to stack into a tower. Anything can be created with these items.

DESCRIPTION: As with any activity, parent needs to sit initially with child and show her how to build a tower and put smaller containers into bigger ones. The important part of this is activity is the talking between you and your child. Such words as on, under, over, and below, as well as color, size, shape, and number words, can be learned by your child during this activity. Asking questions is very important for toddler's problem-solving development: "Where can we put this red block to make the tower larger? What will happen if we put this large green block on top?" Even if your child can't yet talk or formulate answers, ask the questions anyway, and answer yourself: "Would putting the red block on top make the tower taller? Let's try it." Toddlers will enjoy the cause and effect of pushing the tower and watching it fall over. Once your child has experienced this activity with an adult, he or she will happily play with the blocks and containers independently for short periods of time.

ACTIVITY: Choo Choo Chatter
SKILLS: Language development, balance, gross motor movements
WHAT YOU NEED: Plastic laundry basket or a push toy, favorite stuffed animals, books, or toys to put in the basket.
PREPARATION: Get your laundry basket and fill with some of your toddler's favorite toys.
DESCRIPTION: At about nine months your baby will start trying to pull himself up. He will enjoy holding on to a basket or push toy to follow you around the house. Spread her toys around the living room floor and show her how to scoot around either on her knees or standing, picking up her toys, putting them in the basket and making choo choo train sounds. This activity will take on new interest every time you change the contents of the basket.

ACTIVITY: Poem Paste-Ups
SKILLS: Language development plus some hand and body movement
WHAT YOU NEED: Photocopy or write on a piece of paper several of your favorite poems or songs from books you have read aloud.
PREPARATION: Tape poems to the wall, door, or piece of furniture in language play area or any place you spend time with your toddler.
DESCRIPTION: Sit with your toddler and read the poems accompanied by hand or body movements. Encourage other members of family to read the poems when toddler is near them. Before you know it, she will be saying the poems or mimicking the movements on her own when she is near the poems. Switch poems as often as necessary or every two

weeks or month. Save the poems and put in a folder, a lightweight binder, or in a journal. You can also make a little book out of them for baby's bookshelf, so she can refer to the poems and "read" them on her own.

Toddler looks at familiar poems that Mom has read to her, copied, and pasted on the door.

ACTIVITY: Phone Fun

SKILLS: Language development, hand movement

WHAT YOU NEED: Optional: two old phones, or use your hands as pretend phones

PREPARATION: Show your toddler how to use her hand near her ear with thumb on the ear and pinky near the mouth (or any approximation of this hand signal) to imitate a phone.

DESCRIPTION: Both of you pretend you are talking to each other over the phone. Teach her how to have a conversation and use her words (and babbles) to communicate. Soon she will be mimicking what you say and learn how to take turns by waiting for you to respond. After she is adept at this activity, mom can be in the kitchen or elsewhere while baby is in her play area pretending to have a phone conversation by using a discarded phone or her hands. Also mom could communi-cate from a distance with baby by calling out a couple of "ding-a-lings," so baby can "answer" her phone, and have a conversation.

While Mom is cooking dinner, toddler pretends to talk on the phone and Mom talks back.

You can also use this ac-tivity, using your hands as phones, while shopping or anywhere else where there are no toys to keep baby busy.

ACTIVITY: High Chair High Jinks (a medley of high-chair ac-tivities for the twelve- to twenty-four-month child)

SKILLS: Language development, problem solving, and fine motor movements

WHAT YOU NEED: High chair, small stuffed animals, sponges, small plastic cup, egg carton, tray with ½-inch edge, cereal or other munchies, larger items that can be sorted in egg carton with or without closeable lid. Make sure none of the items are a choking hazard. For storage and organization, you may also want to get empty plastic baby wipe boxes, plastic food containers with lids, or sealable plastic bags in which to put the objects. Each of the following objects will go in a separate box or plastic bag: shoelaces, pipe cleaners, wikki stix (colored wax sticks that can be bent into different shapes, available at craft stores), clothes-pins that little toddlers fingers can press open.

PREPARATION: Although most of the time your toddler will be on the go, you'll sometimes need to be sure exactly where she is while you are preparing something that needs more of your attention. These activi-ties are perfect for those busy times. Place your toddler in her high chair near where you are working. Whatever activity you choose, first show her how to do it, and do it with her until she's able to do it on her own. Use your discretion when selecting the activity. For example, if your toddler likes to mouth things you might not want to use the wikki stix until she's older.

DESCRIPTION: The following high-chair activities should be introduced one at a time. Model to your toddler exactly how to use the objects. Once introduced, you will have the materials available to use over and over again. Varying the materials slightly will make an old activity appear as an entirely new activity: Use regular shoelaces, later switching to curly shoe laces, or go from pipe cleaners to wikki stix.

- *Clothespins*: Show toddler how to pinch open the clothespins and attach them to kitchen towel, favorite blanky, stuffed animal ears or tails, the sides of a plastic bowl, or on to each other.

- *Shoelaces*: Show your toddler how to wind around stuffed animals, dolls, trucks, empty plastic water bottle, a dish towel, or wooden spoon.

- *Pipe Cleaners (Wikki Stix)*: Show your toddler how to make shapes, hook one on to another, twist, or wrap around things like a spoon or doll.

- *Egg Carton Sorting*: Give your toddler a little bowl of cereal, minicrackers, or munchies. Show your toddler how to place items in the twelve empty egg cups. Show her how to shut the box and shake it (expect contents to land on floor every so often). When toddler is young, she won't understand yet how to sort items separately, but she'll just enjoy picking out objects and placing them in an empty egg carton. You can still model placing minicrackers in one egg cup and cereal in another.

- *Sponge Squeezing*: This activity involves using sponges to absorb water and squeezing it out. Fill tray with enough water to soak sponges. Show toddler how to rub sponges on surface of tray to soak up water. Then show her how to squeeze the water out onto the tray or small plastic cup. Toddler will eventually pour water from cup onto tray. You can also show her how to use an eye dropper to suck up water.

Parent Support System

In some cultures parents have access to a variety of family and community members to help them raise children. But in the United States new parents can often be isolated, lonely, and on call twenty-four hours a day. It doesn't have to be that way if you think about it and plan ahead. Identify the people among your neighbors, relatives, and friends who would be able to help you periodically so you could catch your breath and get a few things done. The purpose of this is for your child to be in the company of and interact with a real communicative person instead of the television. The people you identify could help baby do the activities in this chapter, as it is difficult for babies before age two to play independently for an extended period of time. They lose interest quickly if there is no one talking with them or leading them in play.

We are not talking about occasional babysitters for when you need to go out at night, go shopping, or do some work during the day. We're talking about getting someone scheduled in to help you for a shorter period of time on a regular basis. For example, a fifth-grade neighbor could come over on Tuesdays and Thursdays after school for an hour to play with your baby, using some of the activities listed above. Imagine what you could get done at home during that time. You don't have to worry because you will be right there at home supervising. However, you would have to invest the time up front in the preparation and training of the fifth grader so he or she would understand how to play and talk to your baby at the same time. A typical fifth grader might love to earn a little extra money.

The key is to schedule someone in so you can rely on him or her. A grandparent, who wants to have a regular visitation and good relationship with their grandchild, could be scheduled for another day of the week. Grandparents appreciate being needed, and they can communicate with baby while taking a walk or other activity. An hour a couple times a week is just right for many grandparents who may tire easily for longer periods. Any of these helpers can be taught to read aloud to your baby using the suggestions in Chapters 3 through 8.

Another alternative is to work out a trade with a parent of an infant around the same age as yours. You can make an arrangement where you take turns coming to each other's homes at designated times, so you can each get something important done around the house. You have to agree to relate more to the babies than each other so your baby gets the needed attention. Initially, it will take some effort to set this up, preparing the materials and showing both the mommy helper and the baby how to use them. You may also find that the fifth grader or grandparent doesn't work out for some reason. Then you have to go back to your list of possible helpers and make a few more calls.

There are many creative ways of dealing with time for parents to get some work done around the house while providing baby with meaningful, literacy-building play activities. The best ideas will be those you and your friends dream up that are tailored to your way of life. The energy you give to provide your baby an alternative to television will be well worth it in terms of your own sense of well-being and the kind of language and literacy promoting environment you make available for your baby's first years of life.

CHAPTER 11

Interviews with Parents of Successful Readers

Reading aloud and talking about books is part of the education of the heart, and it is best done in families and around shared stories.

Lucy Calkins with Lydia Bellino,
Raising Lifelong Learners[1]

None of the parents highlighted in this chapter set out to teach their children to read. However, all of their children eventually became early readers as a by-product of the closeness, the quiet times together, the attention, and the verbal interaction shared between parent and child when reading a book. None of the parents thought of purchasing commercial reading programs or phonics games. If parents did any sort of word games such as rhyming, it was spontaneous. They created their own productive and fun ways to promote language when traveling in the car or running their everyday errands, but never followed a sit-down drill or teaching method.

After so much reading aloud, the children naturally and easily became readers themselves, around first grade. It was not the school, but the parents, who "taught" their children to become readers and to develop a love of reading. None of these parents formally taught their children how to read. By establishing a daily read-aloud routine and plenty of conversation, each of the parents provided the building blocks of literacy. In all instances, the

parents made a priority of spending time with their children, with both mom and dad or grandparents involved in read-aloud time. Most parents monitored or limited television watching. In some cases, there was no television at all. If the children did watch TV, parents often sat with them and discussed what they were watching.

For this chapter, we interviewed parents who involve their children in all kinds of conversations. If the parents spoke a language other than English at home, the same principles were at work. Although the cultures represented in the interviews represent only English-speaking and Spanish-speaking parents, the principles that made their children successful apply to all languages and cultures. When it is time for children to learn English, or the official language of the country, they will do so easily if there is a good foundation of the home language first. Learning and speaking more than one language is not confusing to children.

Some people think that in order to succeed in the mainstream society, families must give up the culture and language of their origin. Actually, this is not the case. Some of the most integrated and successful families we've seen are those that have strong connections to their original culture and language. The way they have blended both cultures and languages is by strong participation in the activities of their new mainstream society. For example, they actively participate in places of worship, they take part in their children's sports or scouting activities, and they become involved in their children's schools. If their culture of origin is very different from that of the mainstream, they still maintain their cultural traditions at home. Children that grow up in this type of environment feel proud of who they and their parents are, but also feel good about their place in the mainstream society.

These parents also gave their children a variety of stimulating experiences. They took their children to museums, zoos, and all kinds of excursions in order to expose them to new experiences and new vocabulary. If mom and dad both worked, there was a grandparent or caregiver to provide conversation and read-aloud time. Such was the case of the Mexican grandparent who told his grandson stories about the Aztec Indians. The parents viewed reading time not only as a routine, but also as an opportunity to have intimate moments with their children, free of any outside distractions. Though these moments could take place at any time of day, they often preceded naps or bedtime, when children would begin to wind down and get ready for sleep.

We'd like to share a handful of stories with you taken from real-life experiences parents and grandparents have had reading and telling stories starting in the first months of the babies' lives. Parents can create a reading routine and read in a way that fits into the needs of their own family. These success stories demonstrate that children develop a sense of well-being, emotional stability, as well as academic achievement because parents have given their children quality, one-to-one, loving attention along with the millions of words that come with daily read-louds in the early years of life. These parents didn't wait until their children began preschool, but began reading soon after birth, giving their children a huge advantage in learning how to read. We hope these stories inspire you to begin reading to your baby today.

Shamone's Story

Shamone, age ten, lived with his mother and his grandmother Roxanne until he was seven. Roxanne played a major role in the day-to-day routines of caring for Shamone. The significance of Shamone's reading background is that it demonstrates that language and reading development do not have to come through books, but rather from a rich oral environment. What is important is that babies and toddlers are talked to regularly in a loving, caring manner. Not all of us have the talent or musical background to be able to sing and chant to our babies. But we can talk and pass on the talents and cultural traditions that each one of us has.

Interview with Roxanne

Q: Tell us about the work you do.

A: I am an arts coach and work with teachers in public elementary schools. What that means is that I am a team member with the teacher to develop artistic modes of teaching in the core curriculum. I go into classrooms and model lessons on how visual arts, drama, or dance can be used to teach math, reading, science, and other core subjects.

Shamone and his Grandmother Roxanne.

Q: Tell us how you have been active in the life of your grandson, Shamone.

A: When he was first born, I would make up songs. Every single night, I would hold him, dance with him, and sing. That's how I would get him to sleep. I would sing about his eyes or his toes or just make up silly songs. I write poetry, so I would sing and chant my poems. I would sing about the trees, body parts, or things in the house. As he got a little older and he was able to sit in a shopping cart, probably before he was two years old, we would go on adventures. We would go to the produce section at the grocery store, and I would play games with him to teach him colors and to count. We would be there for a while. I would say, "OK, we need one red apple. Show me a red apple. Now we need a yellow apple. Show me a yellow one. We need a green apple, too. How many do we have?" I would count, "One, two, three. Well, we also need strawberries. What color are those?" I taught him his colors and counting at the store. As he got older, he would name the colors and count as I held the bag open. We also started adding and subtracting. I would say, "I think we need another one. So if we have three apples and I put another in, how many do we have?" It was a lot of fun, and we usually had an audience. People would just be standing around watching and saying, "Wonderful, you must be a teacher."

When he was about six and a half, we started doing math. "How much is a pound? If grapes are 79 cents a pound, let's round it off. Is it closer to 80 or 70 cents? So if we get one pound of grapes, it will be 80 cents. For two pounds, how much would it be?" So we would take out a piece of paper and write it down. There are so many ways to teach children in your regular everyday activities.

Another place we did a lot of talking and learning was in the car. As he got older and was in kindergarten, we would play the letter game. I would choose a letter, and he would say all the words that he could think of that start with that letter. When he was in first grade, his uncle, who is a composer, would make up a song to help him learn a concept. When he understood it, he would make up his own songs. That's the way we have taught him math, using a keyboard. We would give him a beat to try to teach him double numbers (the addition of two numbers that are the same). We would teach him how to write a song, and then he would write his own song to learn how to sing double numbers with chanting and rapping.

Q: At what age did Shamone start reading?
A: He probably started early in the first grade. When he first started reading, he would try to read everything from billboards to cereal boxes. He is now in second grade and enjoys reading chapter books.

Q: Did you read to Shamone?
A: We read all the time. Everybody in our family reads. We love to read. I read to him, and his mother reads to him. As he got older, he would "read" to us. He could not read, of course, but because we read to him, he would point to the pictures and "read" to us. His Mom orders books through the mail. He belongs to a book club and gets books every month. He also receives books as gifts for his birthdays. We have books everywhere—by the bed and on the dinner table. If you leave books around, kids read them.

Andres' Story

In many cultures, children do not experience read-alouds, but instead listen to storytelling that comes from a long oral tradition. Many of us have had this experience, and we became articulate, literate adults. As effective as reading a book, storytelling and an abundance of being talked to gives babies and toddlers the language and attention they need. Such is the case with Andres Mendez, a six-year-old first grader. Andres' first-grade teacher was very impressed with his academic gains during the end-of-the-year testing. Andres participated in the two-way bilingual program. In his classroom ten students were native Spanish speakers and ten were native English speakers. Each group received instruction in their primary language but also in their second language. Andres, a native Spanish speaker, received his formal reading instruction mainly in Spanish. Most of his instruction in English was oral through songs, chants, rhymes, and sharing of books. During the end-of-the-year first-grade testing,

Andres and his Grandfather.

Andres read a grade-level Spanish-language book with fluency and expression. His teacher decided to try a similar book in English, although he had no formal reading instruction in English. She was pleasantly surprised to see that he was able to read equally well in English. This shows that having a strong primary or home language determines how easily a child will succeed in a second language. We talked to his mother to learn about his early experiences, which prepared him so well for a challenging year in a first-grade bilingual classroom.

Interview with Andres' mother

Q: Tell us about your children.

A: I have two children: Andres is six years old, and his sister is two. When Andres was two months old, I wanted to go back to work. My parents agreed to watch Andres while I was at work. My dad does most of the playing and talking with my kids, and my mother feeds and changes them. My dad—my children call him "Tata"—is like a parrot. He just talks and talks. He always talks to the grandchildren about everything. He plays strange verbal games all day. For example, he says numbers out of sequence and has the kids repeat them. I get concerned at times and tell him that he is going to confuse the children. I ask him to say the numbers in order. Dad says, "Don't worry. They won't get mixed up. I just want them to learn to say the numbers." He says things like, "The parrot has a long nose." He wants to see what kind of a reaction he gets from the children. Of course, they say, "No, Tata, parrots don't have long noses, they have beaks." When Andres was three, dad talked to him about gravity, the Aztecs, and other topics that I thought Andres was too young to understand. My dad likes to tell stories, sing songs, and take the children to see the cows and horses.

When Andres was two years old, he could communicate well with us. We spoke only Spanish at home. We did not start speaking English to him until he was four years old. We watched TV in Spanish and read books to him in Spanish. My dad would read him a book over and over until he had memorized it. When "Tata" tried to change the story, Andres would say, "No Tata, that's not what it says."

When Andres started kindergarten, he said, "I want to learn to read in English." I told him that he would, but first he had to learn in Spanish. Andres would try to read the signs in the store windows when we were out driving. "What does it say?" He would ask questions about why the *ph* sounds like an *f* and why the *sh* sounds like it does. So in a sense, Andres has taught himself. We have just been here to answer his questions. We teach him what he is interested in and wants to know. Now, at the end of first grade, he can pick up a book written in Spanish, read it, and interpret it in English to his sister and me.

Andres learned a lot from TV. He likes to watch TV with an adult who can answer his questions. He loves the Discovery and the History channels. He has conversations with me about what he watches with my dad. He is very sensitive. For example, he has watched programs about situations in Africa, and he talks with me about the children not having food or schools.

Q: Tell us about your dad.
A: My dad is 58 years old and was born and raised in Mexico. He moved to the United States when I was a little girl. He only went to school until the fifth grade. He has worked in the fields, as a truck driver, in a restaurant, and in a bakery. He has a lot of life experiences and can do many things. Now that he is retired, he likes to read, watch educational programs, and play with the grandkids.

Q: Was your dad as involved with you when you were a child?
A: No. When I was young, my dad worked long hours and got home late. We spent most of the time with my mother, who had very little school-

ing. I was the oldest and was told that I had to learn English and do well, since I would be the example for my brothers and sisters. I did not have someone to talk to me or to read to me like Andres has, but I had the pressure from my parents to do well in school, and I'm grateful that I did.

Eric's Story

Eric is a five-year-old kindergartner. He has been reading since he was three. At five years, Eric can read "anything." What totally amazed us when we heard him was not that he could read, but *how* he read. He read with fluency and expression at a very fast pace and would stop every couple of sentences to make a comment about what he was reading. His enthusiasm and ability captivated us. Allie, Eric's three-year-old sister, is also on her way to becoming an accomplished reader.

Interview with Eric's Mom

Q: **What did you do to teach Eric to read with such confidence, speed, and comprehension?**

A: When anyone hears Eric read they say, "Wow, what did you guys do?" It's not like we consciously set out to teach him to read. I think part of it is he inherently has something that makes it easy, and also he loves to read. He was very young when he figured this stuff out. We started reading sporadically when he was an infant and read more when he was older and able to sit up and look at the pictures. Then we really got into it and started reading every night. We knew

Eric reads to his sister Allie and his Mom from Shel Silverstein's book, *Where the Sidewalk Ends*, Harper and Row, 1974.

how important it was. His father and I are both readers. We read all the time. In his bedroom, we had a corner where two bookcases came together, and all his books were so low, he could go in there and play—all his books were always there for him. Early on, as he began to crawl, he would pick out a book and come back and sit cross-legged and ready to read. We still follow this routine.

Another favorite activity was to play with the magnetic letters on the refrigerator. We would say the names and sounds of the letters as I prepared dinner or cleaned the kitchen. Both Eric and Allie enjoy playing games in the car. When Eric was three, we would say a word, and then ask him to change the beginning sound and tell us what the new word was. For example, *"Bat*—if you take away the *B* and add a *C,* what is the new word?" Eric could do this in his head. We would also ask him to change the last letter of a word to make a new word. We played games like this all the time. At times we were trying to find out how hard we could push him before he could not figure it out. Allie at three can spell *Mom, Dad, Eric, Allie.* She sits in the back seat and is constantly asking how you spell words. Just the other day she was saying, *"Weaf. Weaf. W W Weaf."* I figured she was trying to say the beginning sound of *leaf,* but because she still baby talks, it sounded like *weaf* instead of *leaf.*

Q: What else do you believe has contributed to Eric and Allie's advanced skills in the areas of language and reading?

A: I think an important thing is that I don't work outside of the home. We waited seven years until we were at a point where I didn't have to work. My mother was there for me, and I couldn't imagine having someone else raise my babies. I don't want anyone to put anything in their little heads that I don't have control over.

We always talked to our children using regular adult language. We haven't done any baby talk. Another thing that I think has contributed to their love and enthusiasm for books is that when we first moved to this area, Eric was three years old and Allie was four months old, and we did not have a television. We went one year without cable or a satellite dish. At first I thought we would not be able to survive. I soon found out that I didn't have time to watch TV, anyway. We got into the habit of not watching and had no desire to sit down and watch a TV show. My husband and I hate the commercials on TV, with all that stuff they try to sell to kids. Our children are not exposed to that right now. We now have a TV, but Eric and Allie are limited to about three hours of TV a week. They watch some of the educational shows, but mainly they watch videos. My husband and I don't watch TV.

Q: *How do you think books have enriched their lives?*

A: Well, I know their language ability is very advanced. Eric's talking vocabulary is very advanced compared to his friends. Both Eric and Allie talked in full sentences by the time they were two. We always read to them making the characters voices and using almost exaggerated voice inflections. Eric mimics this and reads the same way, just like an adult. Even when he tells you something that happened at school, the way he structures his sentences is so *"literaturisch."* Eric uses words, phrases, and expressions from books that you would not normally use in everyday conversations.

Q: *Why did you decide to put Eric in a bilingual kindergarten classroom?*

A: (*Note*: In Eric's school, bilingual means that English-speaking students learn Spanish, and Spanish-speaking students learn English. Half the students are Spanish-speaking, and half are English-speaking. This type of bilingual program is possible because in this school district there are only two major languages.)

Although Eric is academically very advanced, we do not believe in skipping a year of school. We wanted Eric to be in a classroom where he could interact socially with peers of his own age. Because Eric has a strong foundation in his own language and had mastered many of the skills taught in kindergarten, we knew that learning some of those skills in a second language would stretch him academically.

Fabian's Story

Fabian is a shy five-year-old kindergartner. He has an eight-year-old sister, Andrea. Fabian is being taught reading and math in Spanish (his primary language) while engaging in diverse oral activities in English. Fabian arrived in kindergarten able to read in Spanish. This interview was done in Spanish with Fabian's mother and was later translated.

Interview with Fabian's Mother

Q: *Did you read to your babies?*

A: When my children were born, my husband and I talked to them all the time. However, we did not read to them when they were babies. We believed it was important to speak in real words rather than cute made-up words, because we knew that whatever words we used, they would learn. I just started working when my youngest was five. Before that, I was at home with my children.

Fabian and his Mother read the Spanish version of *The Little Mouse, the Red Ripe Strawberry, and the Big Hungry Bear* by Don and Audrey Wood, Scholastic Inc., 1994.

Q: Do you have books at home?

A: Yes, we have books at home. Many of them are in English because it's hard to get books in Spanish here in the United States. When my children were little, we would use the English books, but we would not read the text. We would just look at the pictures to talk to the kids in Spanish about what we saw. Now that they are older and can read in Spanish, they sometimes choose books in English and try to read them on their own.

Q: Did you have a specific routine around books at home?

A: We did not have a set routine. When she was very little, my daughter Andrea would pick up a book and make believe she was reading it. She still could not talk but would babble her way through a book as she pointed. I think she was imitating her father, who works at home. He sits at a desk and works with books and writing. From the time they were very little, they would sit up on the desk and grab the papers and books. I think Fabian learned to read earlier than Andrea because he not only saw his father reading, but saw his sister reading the books she brought home from school. They enjoy reading and doing their homework together.

Q: Do your children watch television?

A: Yes, I think Fabian learned some of his English before he started school by watching TV. I believe the TV also had something to do with his reading ability because it's closed captioned for the deaf and has the words typed on the screen. Before Fabian came to school, he watched more TV. Now that he is in school, we don't have as much time because we expect them to do their homework and other activities before they watch TV. And they also go to bed by eight o'clock.

Eric, Jennifer, and Jason's Story

Mary has three children—eleven, nine, and seven years old. Although her oldest began reading at age three, most children with book exposure at home begin reading in kindergarten or first grade. As we stated at the beginning of this book, the purpose of reading to your baby is not to expect that he will become an early reader as a toddler, but to provide abundant language and vocabulary, and instill a lifelong love of reading that is associated with the cuddly warmth of being in your arms, listening to a book. Besides the fact that Mary has made reading important in her own family, she has also made a commitment to helping children who haven't had the advantage of being read to. She volunteers in her children's school, encouraging other children to develop a love of reading.

Interview with Mary

Q: When did your children start reading?

A: My oldest started reading before he was three. Everyone thought that he was just memorizing the Dr. Seuss book words, since they rhyme, but we knew for sure when he was reading his third birthday cards that he was not memorizing. My second child started reading when she was five. All my children were read to beginning at birth. We did not do anything differently. My youngest child also started reading at about five.

Q: What was your family practice for communicating with your children from birth? When did you start reading to them?

A: Since they were born, we always talked a lot to them. We have always had hundreds of

Eric, Jennifer, Jason, mom, and dad.

books in our house. From infancy my children were read the little flip-books that you could get wet or they could drool and chew on. Then we went into the thicker page books. By the time they were six months old and could sit up, we read board books. We would read the same books over and over again. We have always had a reading routine before naps and bedtime. When they got older and outgrew their naptime, they could always go to their room and read. This would give Mommy some quiet time. We always read before they went to bed. They could have as many books as they wanted on their beds. We have pictures of them reading when they have actually fallen asleep holding their books. Even today when we go to the grocery store or to church, they all grab three or four books. Our cars are full of books. They take them everywhere. Even for five-minute trips, they grab books.

Q: Are you and your husband readers?
A: I read more now that the children are older. I probably didn't read much more than Dr. Seuss and magazines when they were smaller. But, that's all I had time for. My husband and I do enjoy reading.

Q: How did you manage with more than one child?
A: There is an eighteen-month difference between my first and second child. I would often be holding the younger child on my lap as I read with the older child. While my oldest was napping, I'd read to the younger one. Sometimes I'd have all three of them sitting together. We would read the same book over and over again and point to the words as we were reading. My oldest has always been very inquisitive. By the time he was two years old, he knew all the states and capitals. So when we were reading, he started asking about words. When I was busy, my older children read to the younger ones.

Josué, Briana, and Cristina's Story

The Garcia family of five lives, along with their grandmother, in the house their grandfather built, which stands alone on the top of a small mountain. Patty, the mother, is a bilingual third-grade teacher in a small rural school about forty minutes from their home. All three children attend this school and are doing well, working above grade level in both English and Spanish.

Interview with Mrs. Garcia

Q: Where were you and your husband born?

A: I was born in Guadalajara, Mexico, and my husband was born in Chihuahua, Mexico.

Josué (ten years old), Patty, Cristina (five), José, and Briana (seven).

Q: When did your family immigrate to the United States?

A: I was brought to the United States when I was eight months old. My husband came to the United States when he was twelve years old.

Q: Did you return to Mexico after you moved to the United States?

A: My father always made it a point to take my six brothers and me back to visit Mexico at least once a year in the summer or at Christmas time. My husband and his siblings stayed in the United States for three years before they started visiting Mexico every year.

Q: What language did you speak at home when you were growing up?

A: We spoke only Spanish because my parents did not know English. Once my brothers and I went to school and we were older we spoke in English among ourselves, but continued speaking in Spanish with my parents. In my husband's home they also only spoke in Spanish.

Q: Given the pressures to speak the dominant English language, how did you help your children preserve their Spanish home language and Mexican culture?

A: When we were first married, my husband and I agreed that once we had children we would speak to them in Spanish. My oldest son Josué did not learn English until he was four years old. Josué did not know his father spoke English until one day when he heard his father speaking to his first-grade teacher. At that point he tried speaking in English to his dad, but my husband refused to answer in English.

My husband is the dominant Spanish speaker in our home. Because of her concern that my son didn't speak English, his preschool teacher pressured me into speaking to him mainly in English. Since then I alternate between English and Spanish with Josué. Thinking back now, I wish I had continued speaking only Spanish to him. I speak only in Spanish to my two younger daughters and intend to keep it that way. I now know that it was not necessary for me to speak in English at home for my son to do well in school. I can see by the example of my own children that by having a strong language foundation in their primary language, the second language can be easily learned at school. I have chosen the bilingual school where I teach and where my children go to school, because they will not have to give up their home language as they learn English. In their school they are taught all subjects in both languages.

Q: Do you think that you maintained your culture and language because of your trips to Mexico?
A: I'm very grateful to my parents for having kept in touch with our home country, and now that we have children, we have taken them to both Chihuahua and Guadalajara. They love it! They feel proud of where their parents are from. At some point Josué has told us that he is from Guadalajara. I love that.

Q: What was your parent's educational level?
A: My father went to school only until first grade. My mother went until third grade. My father learned to read and write when he was older and my mother can read and write, but only at a third-grade level.

Q: What was your father's job?
A: He worked in agriculture. He picked avocados and oranges. It was hard labor. I think seeing him work that hard motivated me to seek a better life. I always did well in school, and my brothers and I knew that to have a better life, we would need to stay in school. My parents really supported us as we went through school.

Q: When did you start reading to your own kids?
A: When I was pregnant I remember reading books about how babies in the womb could hear you singing and reading. So I used to sit and read my parenting books out loud. When my first son was born I went out and bought a bunch of board books in English. I would read them to him, but I would translate them into Spanish, since we had decided to speak and read to him in Spanish. One of his favorite books was *Five Monkeys Jumping on the Bed*. We would read that book over and over

again. One day when he was in first grade, he picked up the same book and said, "Mamá, why is this book in English? You have always read it to me in Spanish." I explained to him that as I read the book I would translate into Spanish, because that is the language we had chosen for him as a baby.

Q: **When you had your second child, did you find it harder to read?**
A: Definitely! At first we would read to the older one while we held the younger one. Later, I would read to one and my husband would read to the other.

Q: **When did you read?**
A: We always read right before bedtime. I always made sure my kids had a bookshelf and different kinds of books in their rooms. As soon as they learned to crawl they could go pick a book and bring it to my husband or me so we could read it to them. One of my most memorable times was when Josué, my oldest, was in first grade. He was beginning to read and he would read to his baby sisters. That I loved! I have many pictures of them reading together.

My husband also tells "make-believe stories" to our daughters. After he reads several books to them, he turns off the light and makes up stories. Sometimes Cristina and Briana are characters in the stories, and sometimes the girls help dad by providing the characters or the problem in the story. My daughters love these stories, and I think it is a great way to get them to make images in their minds. However, sometimes my husband wonders how he will be able to come up with a different story every night, but he does.

Q: **Now that you have three children, are both you and your husband involved in the bedtime reading routine?**
A: Yes, because I have been the English model for my son, I do most of the reading with him. Sometimes I will have him read to his sisters. My husband does most of the reading in Spanish with my two younger daughters. When they are older and have to do more reading in English we will probably switch off. I will read to them in English, and my husband will read in Spanish. My daughters, who are in first grade and kindergarten, love bringing their "book bags" from school and sharing books with their papi (dad). It is their "special time" together.

Q: What role do the television and computer play in your home?

A: We have satellite TV. My children are only allowed to watch certain channels and we have to be there. They don't have a TV in their room. We don't want them to watch TV by themselves. Actually, there isn't much time for TV. My kids are all involved in several activities after school, and we come home late after soccer, baseball, karate, choir, or dance. Usually, we come home, eat dinner as a family, do homework, and then have reading time in bed. Even on Saturdays we are involved in sports, so there is little, if any, time for TV.

Q: Your children started out speaking Spanish, but now that they are in school, are they functioning well in English?

A: Yes, they are all at grade level in English. The strong Spanish language foundation we provided by talking and reading at home has helped them make an easy transition into English. We are also lucky that they go to a bilingual school where they will not have to give up their Spanish. In this bilingual program, they will be taught in Spanish as well as English.

Q: What would you recommend to other busy parents to help their kids do well in school?

A: Have books available everywhere. At your house, your car, and grandma's house. Make it a routine to take your kids to the library and bookstores. Give them books for their birthdays and holidays. Prioritize your time so that reading time is built into the before-bed routine or some other time.

Q: Do your kids see you reading for your own pleasure?

A: Most of the reading I do is with them. I do read to prepare my lessons for school and also when I read the bible to prepare my lessons for Sunday school. So yes, they do see me reading.

Henry, Sofie, Annabelle, and Rebecca's Story

Sue, a mother of four, is originally from England, so she introduced her children to some books that are commonly used in England but not in the United States. Sue's older three girls were early and voracious readers. Her son, Henry, now twenty-two months, is more wiggly than her daughters were, and is therefore more of a challenge to read to. Sue has been very creative in adapting to his ways of getting through books, as can be seen in the examples below of her reading to Henry. Babies and toddlers who are too wiggly to read to are a common challenge for parents. The classic image of a baby passively listening to a story is often not a reality. This doesn't mean you give up on reading. Instead, you find a way to adapt, as Sue and many other parents have.

Interview with Sue

Q: When did you start reading to your children?

A: I have four children. My oldest is eleven now. We started reading as soon as she was born. She would just lie in my arms and listen to the sound of my voice. She just loved to be talked to and read to. I

Henry (two years old), Rebecca (eleven), mom, dad, Sofie (six), and Annabelle (nine).

would read British fairy tales to her, and she would just lie there and enjoy the sound of my voice. As she got older, I would read picture books. My other children were read to before they were even born as they heard me reading to the older children. One thing I've always done is have a time before bed when we read. It doesn't matter if we are away on vacation, if they have friends over, or if we are at Grandma's house. They have a bath, they read, and they go to bed. It's always been a routine before bed. Reading helps all of us get in a calm, restful mood.

Q: How have books enriched their lives?

A: They all love books and have a passion about reading. They seem to have good vocabulary, and they read at an early age.

Q: When did they start reading on their own?

A: By the end of kindergarten, my girls could read simple books. And in the summer before first grade, we would practice, so by the time they were in first grade, they were reading very simple chapter books like *Henry and Mudge* and *Amelia Bedilia*.

Q: How did you work out reading with more than one child?

A: They each would get to pick out a book, and I would read them. They would listen to each other's books. When my eldest was in second and third grade, she would still enjoy the books I read to the younger ones. As soon as my second child learned to read on her own, she really did not want me to read to her. She wanted to read the books her older sister read all on her own. I never knew how much she comprehended. She was very independent. In second grade she was reading chapter books, and now in third grade she whips through Harry Potter. Thick books and small print have never intimidated her. Sometimes it's difficult to help one child individually with their reading because the others compete for my attention.

Q: **With Henry being twenty-two months old and Sofie four years old, when do you get to read the books Henry is interested in?**
A: I read to him during the day while the others are at school. At bedtime, usually Sofie and Henry sit and read with me. The older girls read on their own. The funny thing is that my fifth grader still enjoys reading Sofie's picture books. I think it is relaxing for her.

Q: **Do your older girls read to Henry?**
A: Sometimes. Not as much as I'd like. Henry won't sit very well with them, and they get frustrated with him wanting to hold the book and turn it upside down and not go through the pages in the right order.

Q: **Does your husband read to them?**
A: Yes, he reads to them, too. He reads a little less because he travels a lot and has less time.

Q: **Are you and your husband readers? Do you have lots of books at home?**
A: We always have plenty of books in the house. We have more books than shelves! We routinely go to the library. However, the children don't often get to see us reading, since my husband reads mainly on the airplane when he travels, and I read when they have all gone to bed. We do, however, talk about books and encourage them to do well in reading at school.

Q: **Besides reading to your children, did you ever do anything else to help them learn to read? Did you ever use games or special programs?**
A: Well, I borrowed a phonics game, but we only played it once or twice. We did not seem to find the time for it. We started the first game, and

it was kind of boring, and we never found the time to read the rules to find out how to play. I'm glad I did not buy it. I borrowed it. Scheduling a time to sit and play a game is more difficult than the routine of cuddling before bedtime. The children can get the books off the shelf by themselves and put them back. With the game, if they opened the box, then all the different parts were everywhere, and it was a mess. The game was more formal learning. When we read, they didn't know they were learning; they just thought it was fun.

I have used a series of books from England. It's called *Lady Bug Books*. I like to use these books when my children are beginning to read because these books have real stories, but they are written in very simple, one-syllable words. The fairy tales are my favorites. My daughter Sofie (four years old) just read *Puss 'N Boots*. She just got such a kick out of being able to read the whole story of a book that was quite grown up. The books are actual stories, so the children feel a sense of accomplishment, and yet it does not overstress them. I have found that many books sold here in the United States for very young readers are rather simple books with few words on a page. However, they suddenly throw in a long word that a child can't easily read.

Marissa's Story

Marissa is seven years old and a top student at her school. During our conversation with her parents, we detected that from the beginning, they had valued education because they went to all the school functions and meetings with teachers. Mom and dad both helped out in Marissa's classroom, and they supervised her homework after school.

Marissa's family is representative of many parents who just naturally know the right way to give their children the language they need to develop into successful readers. From the time she was born, her parents spent lots of time face-to-face with Marissa playing and talking. Marissa's parents fostered a love of books through their own respect for education and books. They didn't realize that their everyday regular interactions—like talking, reading together, playing, and not watching too much television—were the foundation of good language and literacy that set the stage for Marissa's current success at school.

Interview with Marissa's Parents

Q: Were books available to Marissa when she was a baby?

A: Yes, we belonged to a baby book club that sent books through the mail. When Marissa was only a few months old, she had plastic baby books that were indestructible and good for teething. We had other books, some with hard covers and pages. We talked about the pictures as we read to her.

Q: Did Marissa watch television?

A: She didn't see TV until shortly before preschool. We monitored TV viewing so that she mainly watched educational films and

Marissa with her parents.

videos. Her toys were also often educational, so she learned her letters and numbers before going to school.

Emily's Story

Emily's story was brought to our attention when her kindergarten teacher asked Caroline to give her a reading assessment. In kindergarten, Emily was reading third- and fourth-grade texts with fluency and expression. Emily's parents, both college graduates, are weekly volunteers in her classroom. Although Emily's mom is in

Emily and Michael with their mom, Lynn.

the above photograph, Emily's dad also participated in this interview.

Interview with Emily's Parents

Q: When did you start to read to Emily?

A: We started reading to Emily right after we brought her home from the hospital. We would spend some quiet time together every day.

Q: What kinds of things did you read to her?

A: We read simple books, beginning books that had to do with colors, or books that would have pictures like a ball, cat, or dog—very simple things. We progressed to Dr. Seuss, going through the rhyming, and later started the *Berenstain Bear* collection. Many of the books we read had been given to us as gifts.

Q: When did you read?

A: We read every night before bed and before naptime.

Q: Did you set out to "teach" Emily how to read?

A: No, we didn't. The way we found out Emily could read is sort of an interesting story. She was about four. She already had been at preschool, and we were starting to see some recognition of words. When you are reading and you are tired, there is a narrow band between consciousness and sleep. When I entered this narrow band, I would start saying things that weren't in the book, and Emily would say, "No, Dad, that's not what it says," and then tell me what it said. The first couple of times we thought, well, we've read this book so many times that she must have memorized it. One day we brought in a new book, and when I hit the same narrow band, she did the same thing. She read the words she had never seen before. That is when we realized she could read.

One thing we have figured out is that she does not have the life experiences to understand some of the older books she is reading. So sometimes she'll have questions, and we have to back up and try to figure out how to put it in her terms. She does not have enough background to really comprehend. So that's why I don't mind sometimes going back to the *Berenstain Bear* collection or other books and rereading them as she gets more experience to understand the older books.

Q: When your son Michael was born, how did you incorporate him into your reading routine?

A: My wife and I would take turns, and each one would take one child. If it was my turn with Emily, Lynn would take Michael. Then, the next night we would switch. We established a very good routine, which I think is really important for kids.

Q: Tell us about the routine?

A: It's similar to that of naps. There is a naptime, and right before naptime, there is quiet time when we read to them. Before bedtime, we go through the bedtime routine—the 'jamas, brushing teeth, and all that. I have my chair and Lynn has hers, and we grab one or the other and sit down to read. As they have gotten older, we allow them to pick out the books. This is good and it's bad—because sometimes you read the same book over and over, and as an adult you need some variety. If one of us is not home for a reason, we would first read to one and then the other, or read Emily's book first to both of them, and then Michael's book to both of them. However, when you have two kids sitting with you, you have to figure out who turns the pages.

Q: Do your kids turn the pages?
A: About the time we found out Emily was reading, we started having her turn the pages. Michael is four now and can pick out many of the words. He likes to turn the pages. However, a lot of times you have to tell him when you are at the end of a page. Sometimes he'll say, "No, I'm not ready," because he is still looking at the pictures.

Q: Some people say they feel silly reading to an infant because there is no response.
A: No, I enjoyed our time together. It just gave us some time. As they got older, it became more enjoyable. But initially no, it was a special quiet time trying to settle them down as well as giving us a little time to unwind from the day. I enjoyed it from the very beginning, and I still do. With Emily already reading on her own, she won't let me read to her as often. She'd much rather read to us. She is more into the chapter books, which she and Lynn will take off the shelf and read.

Emily will let Lynn read to her, but I don't get in the middle of a chapter book because of the continuity and knowing where it's at. So when it's my turn to read to Emily and she is in the middle of a chapter book, I pick up another book, maybe one we've gone through before, to read with her.

Q: When you read to your children, do you hold them on your lap?
A: We both have recliners, and they sit on our lap. Emily is getting big enough so that it is more comfortable just sitting on the sofa with her beside me. Sometimes we'll both lie on the floor and read.

Q: Was it more difficult to read when the second child came along?
A: I don't think it is more complicated. I just think you have to realize these are two children, and you have to spend time with each one. You

have the same amount of time, but you have to say what a priority is. Some of the other things don't need to get done. The other thing that has contributed is that they don't watch TV other than videos. We allow one or two videos a week, *Sesame Street* and *Barney*. We don't just park them in front of the TV and let them go. It's mesmerizing. Once in a while I've gotten busy and they've been in front of the TV too long and I go turn it off. But they don't scream and holler like I remember doing when I was a child.

Q: You come from the television generation and watched lots of TV. What made you decide to monitor your child's TV watching?

A: Looking at the quality of the programming. It is too graphic, too real, and too violent. Yes, we watched the *Road Runner*, but today's cartoons are too real, too much like people.

What are some of the tips from the above family's experiences that can help parents in their pursuit of good language and literacy building practices?

- Start reading to babies at birth or shortly after to establish a read-aloud routine.
- Limit and manage television watching.
- Expose children to a variety of stimulating experiences outside their regular home environment. For example, take children to the zoo, library, neighborhood field trips like a construction site, a nearby farm, or any place where they can see something new that encourages different vocabulary than usual.
- Be available to verbally help children make sense of their environment when they ask questions. Talk to your child as much as possible.
- If you speak a language other than the school language at home, involve your family in community activities where you will be using the language of the school before your child gets to school.
- Try not to overschedule the family with too many activities the first few years of life so that you have time to talk and read to your baby.
- Show your babies that you love books and reading. Maintain a library. Even though you have very little time, be sure to allow your children to see that you enjoy books. In this way you are a model for the enjoyment of reading.

CHAPTER 12

Baby Books 101

Practical Tips for Selecting and Making Baby Books

Have you ever gone to the children's section of a bookstore and felt overwhelmed by the number of choices? There are board books, big books, little books, pop-up books, books with noise buttons, flaps, and different textures. There are books about television characters, books based on movies, Dr. Seuss books, Mother Goose and nursery rhyme books, as well as the whole range of holiday books. Understanding the characteristics of books that will strengthen your baby's language development will help guide your decision-making process. Informed book choices will make your read-aloud time more pleasurable and fruitful as your baby learns new vocabulary.

A few well-chosen books of good quality are better than a large number of randomly selected books, some of which may not hold your baby's attention. We hope the following discussion will help you make wise choices that match your baby's language and visual developmental needs.

Before-You-Buy Checklist

❑ Avoid books that are too big and heavy. It's hard to hold a heavy book in one hand while making your baby comfortable with the other hand.

❑ Don't judge a book by its cute cover or title. Read the book from cover to cover to make sure it matches your baby's needs before you buy. (See the "Six Baby Read-Aloud Stages" chart at the front of Chapter 3 for stage-by-stage guidance on types of books).

❑ Make book choices based on language and physical characteristics listed in Chapters 3 to 8 or in the Chapter 3 chart. Use the age recommendations on the back cover of the books only as a suggested guide. Some babies enjoy the same books as older toddlers and some toddlers enjoy books that are recommended as baby books.

❑ Inspect books carefully that are big sellers or have been widely advertised. Are these books appropriate for your baby's present developmental age?

❑ Listen for the rhythm in the book's language to see if it has a cadence and flow you like.

❑ Make sure you enjoy the book. Your enjoyment will be transmitted to your baby.

❑ Try to select books from a variety of genres. Expose your baby to books representing different cultures, especially those of your own heritage. But also choose books to expose your toddler to other cultures.

❑ Check for accuracy and good language when books have been translated from English into other languages, or vice versa.

❑ Check the baby book illustrations. Is there enough variety of colors and textures to keep baby's attention? Or is the drawing or photo of the subject pretty much the same on each page, with muted color values (pastels)? Sometimes the color and variety of textures can be exciting, but the drawing and the words in the book can be too simple and leave very little to talk about with your baby. Book illustrations can also be too complex for babies. Books for baby's first year should be clear, colorful, and simple. They should reflect the meaning of the text. It can be confusing for babies when what they see in the illustrations doesn't match what they hear.

❑ When you select books with gimmicks, different textures, and flaps, be aware that these added features make the books more expensive. With gimmicks, remember that your parentese voice, with its variety of sound effects, will probably maintain your baby's interest over a longer time. But when you do choose gimmicks such as sound effects, limit them to one or two.

Select from a Variety of Genres

Try to provide a variety of genres (types of book based on theme or subject). Traditionally, boys seem to gravitate to nonfiction, based on their interests. Girls most often prefer fiction. But not always. Every child has unique interests no matter whether male or female. Try to choose from among the following genres:

- *Traditional:* Fairy tales, legends, mother goose: These age-old stories are found in every culture. Example: *Hey Diddle Diddle and other Mother Goose Rhymes* by Tomie de Paola.

- *Predictable:* Books with rhyming or predictable endings, which babies or toddlers can memorize. Example: *Where's Spot?* by Eric Hill. Babies soon repeat the word "no" on each page.

- *Nonfiction:* Books that provide accurate information, like books about the body, trucks, or baby animals. Example: *Diggers and Dump Trucks* by Angel Royston.

- *Fiction:* Books that are about fantasy and make-believe characters. Example: *Mrs. Wishy-Washy* by Joy Cowley.

- *Concept:* Books that label things or teach concepts like *over* and *under.* Example: *Caillou, Tell Me Where* by Christine L'Heureux.

- *Alphabet:* Books that feature letters of the alphabet. Select carefully. Example: A classic alphabet book for birth-to-two is *Chicka Chicka Boom Boom* by Bill Martin, Jr., because of its rhythm and rhymes (see Chapter 3), not because it teaches the alphabet.

- *Poetry:* Read through the rhymes in the book to make sure you enjoy most of them. Example: *Hippety-Hop Hippety-Hay* by Opal Dunn.

What Are Board Books?

At any time beginning at birth, you can begin reading board books. Board books are usually small, 8- to 20-page, sturdy cardboard books, available at most bookstores in the children's section. Many have a limited amount of words. A number of popular best-selling children's picture books for ages four and up are now appearing as board books. Not all of these are successfully adapted to a small format and may be too wordy for the smaller board book size. On the other hand, some adaptations, such as *Chicka Chicka Boom Boom,* have abridged text to fit the limited number of board book pages. We prefer the longer complete version, not the board book format, that will be of lasting interest to your child through first grade.

Board books can withstand rough handling and teething as your baby grows. We strongly recommend that you allow your baby to touch, grab, and even bite these durable little books. At about ten months, babies start to mimic the behaviors of readers by sitting by themselves, looking and pointing at illustrations, turning pages, perhaps babbling or laughing at their favorite pages. These behaviors will only take place if babies have been read to on a regular basis and their board books are accessible to them. Babies develop a fondness for favorite books, and board books will last through the first five years and beyond.

Books Based on Videos and Films

Although our recommended book list includes a title with a character from a Public Broadcasting Station cartoon, we didn't include books based on popular family films or videos. We want families to be aware of all the wonderful authors and illustrators available to babies and children outside of the commercial media. As reading teachers, we are disappointed to see so many school-age children who know only the kinds of books or illustrators they have seen in videos or movies.

Books with Gimmicks

In general, books with digital sound effects quickly lose your baby's interest. The reason is that baby's brains are wired for a variety of stimuli. Babies need a constantly changing set of sounds. They quickly figure out that the sounds in these types of books will always be the same. After a couple of exposures babies are ready to move on. Compare this response to that of baby hearing a book like *Barnyard Banter* by Denise Fleming, for example. Every time parents read this simple yet effective book, it catches baby's attention. Why? Because babies never know how you are going to dramatize the sounds. There are always subtle differences in your voice and facial expressions. The words will be the same, but it's how you say them that will maintain baby's interest each time you read it.

Among the books full of gimmicks that we think are high quality is the *Hear and There Book* series. This is a series that can be used starting about eight months and that will grow with your child up through preschool. In addition to the interactive sound buttons, the books offer two large flaps on each color-coded page, a couple of good questions on each page, and clear, realistic photographs along with simple illustrations that aren't too busy. Parents can choose to read the captions to a younger baby along with any necessary discussion. As your baby matures, you can begin to read some of the informative text with vocabulary that includes concepts about farm animals, transportation, night sounds, and birdcalls, the subjects of each of the books in the series.

Toys Based on Children's Books

Stuffed toy characters from books like the *Maisy* series are attractive, but you'll find that your baby's interest in books will outlast his interest in toys. If you have to make a choice between a stuffed doll or a book, skip the toy and buy the book.

For Whom Are Baby Books Really Written?

This is a question you can ask when you're looking for books for your baby. Is there too much text? Are the subjects and ideas too abstract and beyond the scope of your baby's developmental stage? There are a few "children's" books that are gushy and lovely, which we're sure you've seen as gifts at every baby shower. These books have beautiful sentiments that tug at every parent's heartstrings. However, look at the types of books in the "Six Baby Read-Aloud Stages" chart at the front of Chapter 3, and see whether the book has words and illustrations that a baby can relate to and absorb. These so-called children's books have really been written for adults, who buy them assuming that children will like them as much as parents do.

What Determines Your Ultimate Choice of Books to Read to Your Baby?

If some of your favorite books are missing from our list, and you really love these books, and you want your baby to hear them, give them a try. With the exception of newborns, your baby will let you know. All of the books we reviewed in Chapters 3 to 8 have been successfully read to babies. We included only a sampling of books that match your baby's language and physical development. Ultimately your baby's responses, and the way in which you read the book, will determine your choices.

The one exception would be if your child has reached the age of one or two years, and has never been read to before. In that case, your baby may not favorably respond to any books at first, and you may have to introduce reading aloud in small doses until your baby gets used to this activity. In other words, don't give up. We discuss this in detail in the question-and-answer section of the book (Chapter 9).

Where to Find Books for Your Baby

1. **Bookstores:** Specialty children's bookstores, as well as general bookstores and online bookstores, have the largest selections in their children's book sections. Browse through the books, using our list, and take a look. In the process you'll find other books we didn't mention. Make a note of the ones you like. Maybe you can also find these books at a library or discount stores. While you are in the bookstore, check on the times they give read-alouds for toddlers. Online bookstores like Amazon.com give the option of purchasing a new or used book when available. Sometimes used baby books can get pretty grungy if they have been slobbered and teethed on. Sometimes they look like new.

2. **Library:** Get to know your local children's books librarian. Librarians are very knowledgeable and they love books. If they don't have many baby books, show them this book and ask them to purchase some of the books in our recommended lists. Also ask librarians for their schedule of read-alouds for babies and toddlers.

3. **Retail and Discount Stores:** We have been surprised at the number of quality board books, many on our list that we found at some discount stores.

4. **Garage Sales:** You never know what you'll find at garage sales. Some teachers have filled their classroom libraries with garage sale finds.

5. **Trading:** Parents with different-age children may give or trade books, just as you do with toys and maternity and baby clothes.

6. **Grandparents, Relatives, or Friends:** If relatives want to give gifts, give them a list of books you would like. Books are usually less expen-

sive than toys or clothes, and they are easy to buy and mail. They also hold baby's interest for a longer time.

7. **Birthday Parties:** For your baby's one- or two-year birthday celebration, create a party around characters or a theme of a book. Instead of gifts, ask parents to bring a book to exchange with other children. You can also give board books to each child as party favors.

8. **Scholastic or Troll Book Fairs:** Even if you don't have a child in school yet, call your local elementary school and ask when they will be having their book fair (a way for the local PTA to raise funds). This is an inexpensive way to buy new books. Many of the books on our list can be purchased for $3 or less through these fairs.

9. **Catalogues:**

   - *Scholastic Book Club Catalogs:* Call your local elementary school and ask if you can drop by and pick up some Scholastic catalogs. There is one for each age range. The kindergarten–first-grade catalog will have some of the titles we mention, along with other books that are appropriate for babies. Like the book fair books, catalog books can be ordered at reasonable prices.
   - *Chinaberry Catalog:* (See the Additional Resources section at the back of the book for address, website, and telephone.) We love this catalog for its wonderful descriptions of books for all ages. There is even a page of ideas on how to read to the very young. Some of the books on our list are reviewed here, with photos and prices included. Books are divided into categories of board books, on up through increasing levels of difficulty and interest.

10. **Superstores:** You never know what you'll find at superstores like Wal-Mart or Costco. Their stock changes often. If you shop at this type of store, stroll down the book aisles and check out what they have.

11. **Foundations:** There are agencies and foundations that provide books to preschools or parents who lack funds to acquire enough books to provide children with the read-alouds they need to hear to develop language and literacy. (See the Additional Resources section at the back of the book.) Supporting all children in their quest for literacy is the responsibility of every citizen.

How to Create Your Own Customized Baby Books

You're probably thinking, "They're telling me I not only have to read baby books, but now I have to make them too!" Don't worry, we're not suggesting that the books you create be made to sell in bookstores or be of scrapbooking quality. We know someone who is a scrapbooking expert, a sort of Martha Stewart perfectionist, who started a beautiful ABC photo book for her six-month-old son. Her son is now in kindergarten, and she's only on B. So far, the A and B pages are beautiful works of scrapbooking art, but her son has not yet been able to enjoy it.

The most valuable benefit of making customized books for your baby is being able to read aloud together about experiences and family members in your own personal environment. Imagine when your baby sees family members, favorite animals, foods, or herself as the star of your very own book! Although it may take a little extra effort to make your own baby book, you'll feel rewarded when you see your baby's reactions. It also gives your baby the opportunity to revisit a memorable experience, like going to the zoo or a birthday party. Your baby will hear the vocabulary repeated, and this will help him make these words his own.

It's better to have several books with six to ten pages than one fat book with twenty pages. It's easier for your baby to handle, and it's hard to fill twenty pages at one time. After five months or so, your book will have plenty of handling, which is why some parents have the pages laminated at a print shop. However, laminating can be expensive. If you have access to a digital camera and printer, you can print out your pictures (even on regular paper) knowing that if the pictures get handled by little hands, you'll still have them available in your camera or computer for your baby's photo album. You can even have the book bound at your local copy shop using inexpensive comb binding.

Samples of some homemade books.

Use the "Six Baby Read-Aloud Stages" chart from the front of Chapter 3 to help you determine the type of book to make that is best for your baby's developmental stage. For example, a newborn is not ready to appreciate pictures of family and friends. Your baby's vision will be more developed after four months when they'll be able to enjoy more details. At twelve to eighteen months, you could make a book that includes questions like, "Can you find Kitty?"

The following directions can be used to create quick and easy books for your baby. Parents, grandparents, or friends can also easily make books for babies. We recommend starting with a very simple 5- or 6-page book that can take as little time as a half hour to make. Baby will not know the difference between a simple, easy book and a time-consuming, artsy book. If you choose to make a beautiful work of art, you are making it more for yourself than for baby. The books we describe here are disposable, and may not last long unless you laminate them. They will provide hours of fun read-alouds for you and your baby!

Possible Subjects for Your Personalized Baby Books

- Memorable experiences like visiting the zoo, going to grandma's house, visiting the grocery store, a trip to the pet store, going to the beach, park, or the doctor.

- Monthly diary of development (a picture for each month, and then a birthday picture for baby's first birthday).

- Photos of family members.

- A collection of pictures of baby's interests, such as cars and trucks, animals, or princesses, cut out of toy store catalogues or newspaper ads.

What You Need to Make Simple Baby Books

FUN IDEAS AND MORE!

- For a fast and simple book, buy a ready-bound journal at a dollar discount store.
  (Note: We don't recommend plastic books designed for babies that you slide photos into, because many are made with PVC [polyvinyl chloride] that emits fumes known to be unhealthy for babies and children).

- Most of the booklets you'll find will have too many pages, and they won't be durable enough. Here's what you can do: glue five or six pages together using a glue stick. If you buy some different-colored tape, you can take the glued pages and make a border with the colored tape. Use different-colored tape (electrical, about ¹/₂ inch) for each set of glued pages. Now your book will have thick pages on which you can glue photos and write captions.

- Another way to make easy baby books is get two manila folders, cut in half to create eight sturdy pages you can join together by using a hole punch, and weaving yarn or a ribbon through the holes to make a colorful binding.

- For a book that you have comb bound at a copy shop, you will need to buy some heavier colored or white construction paper, or quality card stock. We like comb binding because the book can open and lay flat, making it more manageable for you and baby when reading.

- Be careful about the type of marker or pen you use. Sharpie pens, though permanent, are toxic. Nontoxic water-soluble markers will smear when your baby puts the book up to his mouth. So perhaps a ballpoint pen would be best here. If you laminate, you can use any type of pen or medium for drawing and designs you want.

- Photographs. Use photos of your baby's toys, family, or personal experiences to make your book completely personalized and more meaningful. If you are so inclined you could add shapes like yellow rubber ducks, boats, and cars at scrapbooking stores.

- Catalogue or newspaper cut-outs. When you know what your baby's interests are, you could make a simple book around the subjects of

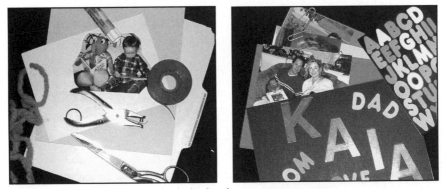

Various materials used to make baby books.

cars, trucks, baby dolls, zoo animals, pets, etc. You can either tear or cut along the edges of the subject. It doesn't have to be exact.

MATERIALS NEEDED

- Scissors

- Hole punch (optional)

- Glue stick

- Colored tape (optional)

- Papers or manila folders

- Pens or crayons

- Photos or pictures

WHAT TO DO

1. Select theme or topic and collect or take photos to use in your book. If you want to be fancy, you can cut or tear the photos around the subject or make into hearts or circles. You can embellish any way you wish, and be as creative as time allows.

Page from homemade book of baby's first birthday.

2. You have the choice of leaving the pictures wordless, adding single-word labels, or writing a short sentence or two. It's best not to write too much text.

3. Glue the pictures on the pages in the order you want them.

4. Read your creation to your baby. You may enjoy reading a book you've made more than many of the books you've been reading to your baby. When you use your parentese voice to talk about the pictures, you'll be thrilled by your baby's positive responses, and be happy when he wants you to read it again and again. When your baby is around one year old, you can ask, "Who's that?" pointing to baby, and listen to your baby say her name. The books will be a delight to share time and time again.

Notes

Introduction

1. Betty Hart and Todd Risley, *Meaningful Differences in the Everyday Experience of Young American Children* (Baltimore: Brookes Publishing, 1996), pp. 160, 198, 199.
2. Marian Diamond and Janet Hopson, *Magic Trees of the Mind* (New York: Penguin Putnam, 2000), p. 37.
3. Ibid, p. 105.
4. Rima Shore, *Rethinking the Brain, New Insights into Early Development* (New York: Families and Work Institute, 1997), p. 19.
5. Diamond and Hopson, *Magic Trees of the Mind*, p. 37.
6. Ibid, p. 38.
7. Ibid, p. 105.
8. Jack Prelutsky, *Read-Aloud Rhymes for the Very Young* (New York: Alfred A. Knopf, 1986), Introduction.

Chapter 1

1. Roberta Michnick Golinkoff, Ph.D., and Kathy Hirsh-Pasek, Ph.D., *How Babies Talk* (New York: Penguin Books, 2000), pp. 9, 51–52.
2. Jane Yolen, Laurel Molk, illustrator (New York: Little, Brown and Company, 2000), p. 9.
3. Betty Hart and Todd Risley, *Meaningful Differences in the Everyday Experience of Young American Children* (Baltimore: Brookes Publishing, 1996), pp. 192, 159, 160, 198.
4. Donald P. Hays and Margaret G. Ahrens, "Vocabulary Simplification for

Children: A Special Case of 'Motherese,'" *Journal of Child Language* 15 (1988): 395–411.

5. Anne E. Cunningham and Keith E. Stanovich, "What Reading Does for the Mind," *American Educator*, American Federation of Teachers (Spring/Summer 1998), p. 4.

6. Hays and Ahrens, *Journal of Child Language* 15 (1988), pp. 400–401.

7. Ibid, p. 401.

8. J. David Cooper and John J. Pikulski, *Wonders, Houghton Mifflin Reading* (Boston: Houghton Mifflin, 2003).

9. Lise Eliot, Ph.D., *What's Going on in There? How the Brain and Mind Develop in the First Five Years of Life* (New York: Bantam Books, 1999), pp. 386–387.

10. Jim Trelease, *The Read-Aloud Handbook*, Fifth Revised Edition (New York: Penguin Books, 2001), p. 197.

11. Pamela C. High, MD, et al., "Literacy Promotion in Primary Care: Can We Make a Difference?" *Pediatrics* 105, No. 4 (April 2000): 927–934; Dr. Wendy S. Masi and Dr. Roni Cohen Leiderman, editors, *Baby Play: 100 Fun-Filled Activities for You and Your Baby to Enjoy* (New York: Barnes & Noble Books, 2004), p. 127.

12. Marie M. Clay, *By Different Paths to Common Outcomes* (York, Maine: Stenhouse Publishers, 1998), Chapters 8 and 9.

13. Cunningham and Stanovich, "What Reading Does for the Mind," p. 4.

Chapter 2

1. Lise Eliot, Ph.D., *What's Going on in There? How the Brain and Mind Develop in the First Five Years of Life* (New York: Bantam Books, 1999), p. 341.

2. Marian Diamond and Janet Hopson, *Magic Trees of the Mind* (New York: Penguin Putnam, 2000), p. 88.

3. Eliot, *What's Going on in There?* p. 248.

4. Ibid, p. 247.

5. We relied on the following authors for information on parentese:
Lise Eliot, *What's Going on in There? How the Brain and Mind Develop in the First Five Years of Life* (New York: Bantam Books, 1999), p. 387; Bénédicte de Boysson-Bardies, *How Language Comes to Children From Birth to Two Years* (Cambridge, Mass.: MIT Press, 1999), pp. 81–85; Roberta Michnick Golinkoff and Kathy Hirsh-Pasek, *How Babies Talk* (New York: Penguin Books, 2000), p. 4; *Brilliant Beginnings* (Long Beach, Calif.: Brilliant Beginnings,

1999), pp. 40–42; J. Madeleine Nash, "Fertile Minds," *Time* Magazine (February 3, 1997), pp. 54–55.

Chapter 3

1. We relied on the following authors for information on language and physical characteristics in Six Stages Chart and in Chapters 3 to 8:
William Sears, M.D., and Martha Sears, R.N. *The Baby Book* (New York: Little, Brown and Co., 1993); Marian Diamond and Janet Hopson, *Magic Trees of the Mind* (New York: Penguin Putnam, 2000); Roberta Michnick Golinkoff, Ph.D., and Kathy Hirsh-Pasek, Ph.D., *How Babies Talk* (New York: Penguin Books, 2000); William Staso, *Neural Foundations, What Stimulations Your Baby Needs to Become Smart* (Santa Maria, Calif.: Great Beginnings Press, 1995); William Staso, *Brain Under Construction: Experiences That Promote the Intellectual Capabilities of Young Toddlers* (Orcutt, Calif.: Great Beginnings Press, 1997).
2. The book dad is reading is *The Baby's Lap Book* by Kay Chorao, copyright (c) 1977, 1990 by Kay Chorao. Used by permission of Dutton Children's Books, a division of Penguin Young Readers Group, a member of Penguin Group (USA) Inc., 345 Hudson Street, New York, N.Y. 10014. All rights reserved.

Chapter 4

1. Lise Eliot, Ph.D., *What's Going on in There? How the Brain and Mind Develop in the First Five Years of Life* (New York: Bantam Books, 1999) p. 209.
2. The book the mother is reading is *Bunny's First Snowflake* by Monica Wellington, copyright © 2000 by Monica Wellington. Used by permission of Dutton Children's Books, a division of Penguin Young Readers Group, a member of Penguin Group (USA) Inc., 345 Hudson Street, New York, NY 10014. All rights reserved.

Chapter 5

1. Roberta Michnick Golinkoff, Ph.D., and Kathy Hirsh-Pasek, Ph.D., *How Babies Talk* (New York: Penguin Books, 2000), p. 193.

2. The book that mother is reading is *The Lifesize Animal Counting Book*, A Dorling Kindersley Book, 1994.

Chapter 6

1. Gerald Coles, *Reading Lessons, The Debate over Literacy* (New York: Farrar, Straus and Giroux, 1998), Chapter 3.
2. The book that mother is reading is *Carl's Afternoon in the Park*, written and illustrated by Alexandra Day, Green Tiger Press, 1991.

Chapter 7

1. Roberta Michnick Golinkoff, Ph.D., and Kathy Hirsh-Pasek, Ph.D., *How Babies Talk* (New York: Penguin Books, 2000), pp. 192, 193.
2. The book mother is reading is *Off We Go!* by Jane Yolen, illustrated by Laurel Molk, Little, Brown and Company, 1999.

Chapter 8

1. Roberta Michnick Golinkoff, Ph.D., and Kathy Hirsh-Pasek, Ph.D., *How Babies Talk* (New York: Penguin Books, 2000), p. 193.
2. Ibid, pp. 138, 139.
3. The book dad is reading is *Bus Stops* by Taro Gomi, Chronicle Books, 1985.

Chapter 9

1. William Staso, *Neural Foundations: What Stimulations Your Baby Needs to Become Smart* (Santa Maria, Calif.: Great Beginnings Press, 1995), p. 39.
2. Marian Diamond and Janet Hopson, *Magic Trees of the Mind* (New York: Penguin Putnam, 2000), p. 133.
3. Staso, *Neural Foundations,* p. 8.
4. Roberta Michnick Golinkoff, Ph.D., and Kathy Hirsh-Pasek, Ph.D., *How Babies Talk* (New York: Penguin Books, 2000), p. 32.
5. Mem Fox, *Reading Magic, Why Reading Aloud to Our Children Will Change Their Lives Forever* (San Diego: Harcourt, 2001), p. 17.

6. Jim Trelease, *The Read-Aloud Handbook*, Fifth Revised Edition (New York: Penguin Books, 2001), p. 28.

7. Bertha Pérez and María E. Torres-Guzmán, *Learning in Two Worlds: An Integrated Spanish/English Biliteracy Approach* (New York: Longman, 1992), p. 42.

8. Golinkoff and Hirsh-Pasek, *How Babies Talk*, p. 23.

9. Ibid, pp. 23–25.

10. Diamond and Hopson, *Magic Trees of the Mind*, p. 109.

11. Trelease, *The Read-Aloud Handbook*, p. 197.

12. Ibid, Chapter 8.

13. Diamond and Hopson, *Magic Trees of the Mind*, pp. 216–227.

14. Victoria J. Rideout, Elizabeth A. Vanderwater, and Ellen A. Wartella, "Zero to Six: Electronic Media in the Lives of Infants, Toddlers and Preschoolers," *Henry J. Kaiser Family Foundation and the Children's Digital Media Centers (CDMC)* (October 2003), p. 6. Available at www.kff.org.

15. Diane E. Levin, *Remote Control Childhood? Combating the Hazards of Media Culture* (Washington, D.C.: National Association for the Education of Young Children, 1998).

16. Steve and Ruth Bennett, *365 TV-Free Activities You Can Do with Your Child* (Holbrook, Mass.: Adams Media Corp., 1996).

17. David McPhail, *Fix-it* (New York: Dutton Children's Books, 1984).

18. Patricia Logan Oelwein, *Teaching Reading to Children with Down Syndrome: A Guide for Parents and Teachers* (Bethesda, MD: Woodbine House, 1995), p. 2.

19. Dorothy Butler, *Cushla and Her Books* (Boston: The Horn Book, 1980).

20. Trelease, *The Read-Aloud Handbook*, 29.

Chapter 10

1. Victoria Rideout, Elizabeth Vanderwater, and Ellen Wartella, *Henry J. Kaiser Family Foundation and the Children's Digital Media Centers (CDMC)* (Fall 2003), p. 8. Available at www.kff.org.

2. Jim Trelease, *The Read-Aloud Handbook*, Fifth Revised Edition (New York: Penguin Books, 2001), p. 197.

3. Dimitri A. Christakis et al., "Early Television Exposure and Subsequent Attentional Problems in Children" *Pediatrics* 113, 4 (April 2004): 708–713.

4. Facts and Figures About Our TV Habit, www.tvturnoff.org.

5. Ibid.

6. Gabor Maté, M.D., *Scattered: How Attention Deficit Disorder Originates and What You Can do About It* (New York: Penguin Putnam, 2000), p. 175.

7. Anne E. Cunningham and Keith E. Stanovich, "What Reading Does for the Mind," *American Educator*, American Federation of Teachers (Spring/Summer 1998), p. 2.

Chapter 11

1. Lucy Calkins and Lydia Bellino, *Raising Lifelong Learners* (Reading, Mass.: Addison-Wesley, 1997), p. 43.

Additional Resources

Useful Websites

Zero to Three

This site is the most extensive resource for parents and researchers interested in all aspects of the development of children from birth to three. Topics such as brain and literacy development are given an in-depth treatment. Research articles and brochures can be downloaded. Spanish resources are also included. Of particular interest to us is the link, "Getting Ready for School Begins at Birth." The "Early Literacy and Brain Wonders" link gives you all the information you need on how literacy begins at birth in relation to the developing brain.
www.zerotothree.org

Beginning with Books, Center for Early Literacy

This organization coaches parents, grandparents, and caregivers about the value of reading to babies and preschoolers, especially those at greatest risk. "Beginning with Books" connects hundreds of volunteers and children for one-on-one read-alouds. Check out their "Best Books for Babies" link.
www.beginningwithbooks.org/list.html

Trelease on Reading

Jim Trelease is the original read-aloud guru. We love Jim Trelease. He has done more for literacy progress than any other individual. His wonderful book, *The Read-Aloud Handbook*, has sold over two million copies, and its

fifth updated edition was published in 2001. You can check the contents of his 2006 edition on his website, which is full of useful information related to literacy. You'll also find lists of children's books, plus research on topics such as TV and its effect on reading.
www.trelease-on-reading.com

Reach Out and Read

A nonprofit literacy organization affiliated with Boston University School of Medicine, Reach Out and Read promotes early literacy through pediatricians informing new parents about the importance of reading to their babies. Doctors give new books to children at each well-child visit from six months to five years. Physicians and pediatric nurses give parents developmentally appropriate instructions on how to read to their babies.
www.reachoutandread.org

Reading Is Fundamental

Reading Is Fundamental is the oldest and largest nonprofit organization in the United States that benefits literacy development. Each year it provides 4.5 million children in need with millions of free books and literacy resources. They train community volunteers in every state. They are funded by the U.S. Department of Education, corporations, foundations, community groups, and individual contributions.
www.rif.org

Read to Your Baby

This easy-to-use website is of interest to anyone interested in the language and literacy development of babies from birth to two. Created by two reading specialists, the authors of *Baby Read-Aloud Basics,* it offers a comprehensive look at most of the issues involved in reading to babies for today's busy parents. Among the topics covered are baby book reviews, brief overviews of some of the important research about the benefits of reading to babies, the features of parentese, bilingual issues, and the difference between reading to babies and older children, plus much more.
www.Readtoyourbaby.com

TV Turn Off Network

A nonprofit organization that encourages children and adults to watch less TV to become healthier, more literate citizens, this organization sponsors two key programs: TV Turn-Off Week and More Reading Less TV. It's supported by more than sixty-five organizations, including the American Medical Association, the National Education Association, and the American Academy of Pediatrics. More than 24 million people have participated in Turn-Off-TV week. It provides a list of TV facts and figures supported by research studies.
www.tvturnoff.org

American Speech-Language-Hearing Association

This is the website parents can go to if they are in need of a professional speech and language practitioner to evaluate and provide services for any suspected language disorders. You can go to the home page and click on "Find a Professional," and then locate a certified professional in your area by completing the form prompts.
www.asha.org

Chinaberry, Books, and Other Treasures for the Whole Family

We recommend this website and catalogue because each baby and children's book has been read to children and carefully selected. New parents will find support in their search for Level I books and reading the inviting, informative write-ups on each book. Both the website and the catalogue are easy to use. There is a page at the beginning of the book section entitled *Ideas for Reading Books to Very Young Children,* which new parents will find helpful.
www.Chinaberry.com

Planet Esmé, A Wonderful World of Children's Literature

This is a bountiful site for lovers and aficionados of children's books. It is the creation of Esmé Raji Codell, the author of *How to Get Your Child to Love Reading* and several other books. You'll find an abundance of information about books for babies, grandparent books, great read-alouds, thematic book lists, holiday titles, and books for children of all ages.
www.planetesme.com

A Short Bibliography of Good Resource Books

Calkins, L. and L. Bellino. *Raising Lifelong Learners.* Reading, Mass.: Addison-Wesley, 1997.

Codell, Esmé Raji. *How to Get Your Child to Love Reading.* New York: Workman Publishing, 2003.

Diamond, M., and J. Hopson. *Magic Trees of the Mind.* New York: Penguin Putnam, 2000.

Eliot, Lise. *What's Going on in There? How the Brain and Mind Develop in the First Five Years of Life.* New York: Bantam Books, 1999.

Fox, Mem. *Reading Magic. Why Reading Aloud to Our Children Will Change Their Lives Forever.* New York: Harcourt, 2001.

Gopnik, A., A. N. Meltzoff, and P. K. Kuhl. *The Scientist in the Crib.* New York: William Morrow, 1999.

Hart B. and T. Risley. *Meaningful Differences in the Everyday Experience of Young American Children.* Baltimore: Paul H. Brookes, 1996.

Hirsh-Pasek, K. and R.M. Golinkoff. *How Babies Talk.* New York: Penguin Putnam, 2000.

Newman, S. B., D.C. Celano, A. N. Greco, and P. Shue. *Access for All, Closing the Book Gap for Children in Early Education.* Newark, Del.: International Reading Association, 2001.

Sears, W. and M. Sears. *The Baby Book.* New York: Little, Brown and Co., 1993.

Staso, William. *Neural Foundation: What Stimulation Your Baby Needs to Become Smart.* Santa Maria, Calif.: Great Beginnings Press, 1995.

Trelease, Jim. *The Read-Aloud Handbook, Fifth Revised Edition,* New York: Penguin Putnam, 1995.

Index